BHAKTI

The Philosophy of Sri Chaitanya

The Publication of this Book has been financially supported by the Indian Council of Philosophical Research. The Responsibility for the facts stated or opinions expressed is entirely of the author and not of the ICPR.

BHAKTI

The Philosophy of Sri Chaitanya

Minakshi Sethy

ATLANTIC

PUBLISHERS & DISTRIBUTORS (P) LTD

Published by

ATLANTIC

PUBLISHERS & DISTRIBUTORS (P) LTD

7/22, Ansari Road, Darya Ganj, New Delhi-110002
Phones : +91-11-40775252, 40775214, 23273880, 23275880
Fax: +91-11-23285873
Web: www.atlanticbooks.com
E-mail: orders@atlanticbooks.com

Printed & bound in India by Atlantic Print Services

Preface

Initially, when I thought of choosing this work, I found myself lost in the woods where every tree, every rock, every scenery seemed worthy of deep study and analysis. Myself, being a student of philosophy, I found it impossible to choose the worthy one among the lot of bests. Then, amidst this confusion, my memory drifted back to my childhood days; and the scene of *rasa-lila* and group of people engaging in chanting and dancing in *kirtana*, and regularly taking the various names of Lord *Krsna* madly. That is called as *nama sankirtana*. Though I did not understand anything about the relevance of *nama sankirtana* at that time, I poised myself as a mere observer.

It always intrigued me that what has been the factor, which compels most of the people of my village to present themselves at the *nama sankirtana* with such concentrated devotion and love. Is it the religion as it seems from outside, or does it comprise something more than the religion, such as human relation, love for other or self-introspection? It had taught me that the human race seems generally to be ego-centric, that in truth a human being is nothing but a creation of that super-natural force that can lift himself from the pedestal of a common person to the level of his creator by his own *karma*.

In the year of *navakalevara* of Sri Jagannath of Puri, Odisha, collection of neem log for construction of new idols, we saw everyday on T.V. channels, people paying devotion to the selected tree and the log clad in silk cloth. Are they devotees charged with some super natural feeling or they were made devotees by the media? Doubts arise about the genuiness of ultra-modern *bhakta*s. But there is no such doubt about classical bhaktas, both puranic figures like Dhruv, Prahllad, Uddhav etc. and historical figures like Rupa Gosvami, Madhavendra Puri, Sri Chaitanya, Panchasakhas etc. I have confined my study to the concept of *bhakti* in Vaisnavism, especially in the Philosophy of Sri Chaitanya.

Minakshi Sethy

Contents

1

Introduction: Life and Times of Sri Chaitanya

History says Sri Chaitanya was born in 1486 at Navadvipa (Nadia) of West Bengal. Though the date of birth of Sri Chaitanya has been pointed out by a group of scholars that it is 1485 rather 1486. As far as research is concerned, it requires the findings of both the contemporary literature of Sanskrit and Bengali. Sri Chaitanya was the tenth child of Jagannath Misra and his wife Sachi Devi. Jagannath Misra was a learned pandit of Navadvipa. In the 15th century, Navadvipa was a prosperous town and was a great centre of trade. It was also famous for Medieval Sanskrit literature at the time of Sri Chaitanya's birth. The new system of logic called *Navya—Nyaya* which had its birth in Mithila, had been introduced to Navadvipa before the time of Sri Chaitanya.

Sri Chaitanya's grandfather had migrated from Odisha to Sylhet (at present Bangladesh) about 1451 and then his father from Sylhet to Navadvipa. Thus, the people of Odisha pay their devotion to Sri Chaitanya, thinking always that he helds from Odisha. His father was a Brahmana of religious disposition. He was a Vaisnava of devout faith and pious life. It is also remarked that the mother of Sri Chaitanya was also a daughter of a well-known scholar; because of this, the child Sri Chaitanya began his life as a privileged child. He has inherited the peculiar social advantages of Brahmanahood as well as blessed far more by birth in a home whose mindsets were formed by traditions of scholarship and religious piety.

Miraculous activities are reported to have taken place about Sri Chaitanya that the young Visvambhara or Nimai or Gauranga was not a normal child. One of the activities is that about thirteen months before his birth, his father had felt a divine light enter into his heart and then passing on to Sachi's. And she also saw many gods worshipping her. Soon after the child was born, his parents were surprised to see the small footprints in the room, which showed a clear-cut mark of a banner, thunder, conch, discus, etc. When mother Sachi began to feed the child, she noticed these marks on the boys' feet.

At the age of five, Sri Chaitanya had started his learning in a tol, and at the age of ten, he had become proficient in Sanskrit grammar, and before fifteen, he was adjudged as one of the best scholars of Navadvipa. He seems to have confined his study largely to grammar and logic for which the Navadvipa tols had become famous. According to the tradition, he made a fairly extensive scholastic tour in East Bengal (present Bangladesh), holding disputations and teaching from town to town.

Intellectual Growth

According to the legend, the charm of the boy had not been lost on reaching manhood. Sri Chaitanya was a man of fine presence with unusually fair skin, lustrous eyes and a mass of hair worn long over the shoulders. His personal charm, assured social standing as a Brahmana and his distinction as a promising young scholar in a university made him a scholastic marked figure. No wonder, the Vaisnava leaders grieved that so promising a son of a Vaisnava household should show so little interest in his father's faith. This was not due to any lack of religious influence. As the son of a pious Vaisnava, he had known no other than a religious atmosphere. Direct efforts to influence him were met in a half jesting, half skeptical spirit that betokened little vital interest.

In Indian tradition, we found that there are four stations of life, these are—*Brahmacharya*, *Garhasthya*, *Vanaprastha*, and *Sanyasa*. Out of these four stations or *dharmas*, *sanyasa-dharma* is the last and most important than other stages. Once a person adopts *sanyasa-dharma*, he cannot come back to other *dharma*s. It is also mentioned in the same tradition that only brahmanas can adopt *sanyasa-dharma* by Advaitic tradition.

It is very clear that if a person has bitter experience on his family life, like Ramanuja or he has disgusted experience on his surroundings, like prince Siddhartha or a person fully enjoyed his life in this world what he wants to, is the reason to adopt *sanyasa-dharma*. But these reasons are not the main ground for adopting *sanyasa-dharma* in the case of Sri Chaitanya.

When Sri Chaitanya had gone to Gaya for performing the obsequies for the salvation of his ancestors, he met Isvara Puri, one of the disciples of Madhavendra Puri, a celebrated personage who was the first to introduce the practice of *bhakti* among the *sanyasis*. There he requested him to accept as his disciple and gave him initiation. But Isvara Puri, tried to win him to a devout life. In response, Sri Chaitanya was to pick flaws in the grammar of the Sanskrit texts quoted by the *sanyasis*. This attitude may have been partly a mask to hide an undercurrent of feeling suppressed but stirring. Then Isvara Puri pleased to him and helps him to realize a glimpse of Radha's love for Srikrsna. So, Puri initiated him into the mantra for *Krsna* worship. Sri Chaitanya was immediately transformed. This is the turning point in Sri Chaitanya's life.

Sri Chaitanya decided to accept *sanyasa-dharma* on the ground that when he became a *sanyasi*, everyone would show him respect. Though he admitted that there was no need for him to accept *sanyasa-dharma*, he did so for the benefit of those who might think him an ordinary human being. The main purpose of his accepting *sanyasa-dharma* was to deliver the *mayavadi sanyasis* (the *sanyasis* who admit everything is *maya*). Another reason for this is that he accepted *sanyasa-dharma* to facilitate preaching his devotional cult.

At the time of Sri Chaitanya's *sanyasa vrata*, he was not aware of all the surroundings. His mind was absorbed in Radha's sentiment of separation from Lord *Krsna* and her sympathized anxiety to see Him. The soul in the state of *samsara* is wedded to the body. Renunciation for the Vaisnava meant the breaking of this wedlock and getting wedded to the Lord.

Sri Chaitanya is not a follower of Advaita tradition. He refused the absolutism of *Sankara*. He called them as *mayavadis*. But when he requested Kesava Bharati (one of the followers of Advaita Philosophy) for giving him initiation. He refused him for the following reasons. First, by virtue of *Krsna-prema* he was greater than himself, and next he had not received the willing and full permission of his old mother and youthful wife to abandon them and take to the life of asceticism.

The devotees from Nadia and the local citizens joined to block Sri Chaitanya's decision. By very cleaver persuasion and the intensity of his spirit of renunciation, he was able to overcome the unwillingness of Kesava Bharati. The ascetic at last initiated him into *sanyasa* and gave him the consciousness of *Krsna* in the minds of men.

During the time of Sri Chaitanya, the influence of Sankaracharya (the founder of Monism/Advaita philosophy) in society was very strong. People thought that one could accept *sanyasa* only in the disciplic succession of Sankaracharya. But Sri Chaitanya, not wishing to disturb the social convention, took the renounced order of life from a *sanyasi*. He wants to avoid such a misconception placing himself as an eternal servitor.

The impersonalists, who are followers of Sankaracharya, are generally known as *kasira mayavadis*. Near Varanasi, there is another group of impersonalists, who are known as *saranatha mayavadis*. Factually, both the *mayavadis* as well as any other philosophers who have no knowledge of the spiritual soul are advocates of utter materialism. Actually neither the *kasira* nor the *saranatha mayavadis* accept the principles of the *Bhagavad Gita* due to a poor fund of knowledge. The impersonalists who do not have perfect spiritual knowledge cannot understand the principles of *bhakti-yoga*; they must be classified among the non-devotees who are against the *Krsna* Consciousness Movement. The Chaitanyaites sometimes feel unconvinced by the hindrances offered by these impersonalists, but they do not care about their so-called philosophy. Both kinds of *mayavadi* impersonalists conclude that the subject matter of *bhakti-yoga* is a creation of *maya*, and that *Krsna*, devotional service and the devotees are also *maya*. Therefore, Sri Chaitanya states that '*mayavadi Krsne aparadhi*' means all the *mayavadis* are regarded as offenders of Lord *Krsna*. So, we, the Vaisnavas do not value to their philosophical conclusions. However, expect such quarrel some impersonalists are in putting forward their so-called logic, we defeat them in every respect and go forward with our *Krsna* Consciousness Movement, which is completely spiritual and is never under the control of such *mayavadis*. *Mayavadi sanyasis* neither chant nor dance. Their technical objection is that this method of chanting and dancing is called *tauryatrika*, which indicates that a *sanyasi* should completely avoid such activities and engage his time in the study of Vedanta.

Evidently, Jagannath Misra's home was open to all the wandering Vaisnavas who passed in and out of Navadvipa, so much so that Sri Chaitanya's childhood and youth must have harbored many memories of venerated guests. One such ascetic, whom Sri Chaitanya met years afterward in his travels, had a vivid memory of the devout hospitality of that (Navadvipa) home. All these influences must have made their impression on the young mind of Sri Chaitanya. It helped to form the subconscious store of latent feeling and aspiration.

Sri Chaitanya's transcendental mission is to distribute love of Godhead to everyone. This munificent broadcasting of devotional service is possible only for Lord *Krsna* Himself. Svarupa Damodara Gosvami has described Sri Chaitanya as a combination of *Radha-Krsna*. He is the shelter of the demigods, the goal of the *Upanishad*s, the be-all and end-all of the great sages, the beautiful shelter of His devotees, and the essence of love for the lotus-eyed gopis. The activities of Sri Chaitanya's philosophy of *Radha-Krsna* are vehemently described in the writings of Prabhat Mukherjee. Besides, the colonial writers, like J. Beams, W.W. Hunter has also contributed the views of Sri Chaitanya.

Political, Social and Religious Environment of Bengal

If we take a bird's eye view of the political and social conditions of Bengal in the period (from 11th to 12th century), it was full of chaos and confusion. Sri Chaitanya's advent has produced a far-reaching effect on the religious and social activities of medieval history of Bengal in particular and Eastern Odisha in general. In order to explain how this could be possible, a review of the condition of the religious life and of the social evolution that was going on in this century is essential from many points of view.

Medieval Bengal, more than 500 years ago, was not in social or religious order. Various factors united to produce a state of society commonly looked back upon as the dark period of Bengal history, with the coming of the British rule and order. Because of this, the country was dominated by an alien force both in race and religion. Friction was the natural result. Repression and religious persecution became features of so-called Hindu life. They hated *Hinduism*. Out of the more or less chaotic conditioned left by a disintegrating Buddhism, the Brahmana architects of Hinduism had sought to ensure stability by laying the caste-foundations solid and strong. The domination of the Brahmana over much of society was the crowning feature of this social order. There was no escaping the rule of the Brahmanical hierarchy in all matters of worship.

Excepting among aboriginal cults and the surviving trace of Buddhism, their service as priests was absolutely essential. Their spiritual superiority to all men was firmly established and recognized everywhere, almost divine honor being paid them by many. They alone could teach the sacred law, perform the ancient sacrifices, or conduct the manifold rites and ceremonies essential to Hindu life. This amazing control over the religious life of the people made the Brahmana master more powerful. Since in India, no social fact falls outside the purview of religion.

Irrespective of this Brahmanic control over the religious life, it was at low ebb in Bengal at the time of Sri Chaitanya's birth. The worship of deities hardly above the animistic stage was strongly entrenched in every village. Side by side, they also practiced *tantra*. The ill-effects of the tantric practices left behind by Buddhism and also deep impact in current Hinduism had gone far in the social order, and exercised a peculiarly debasing influence on religious thought.

During this period, there are three cults came to be in scene; *nath-cult*, *dharma-cult*, and *sakta-cult* in order to provide the stabilizing force in the society in the form of the believers of the masses. The *nath-cult*, which was originated at that time and the *dharma-cult* also probably co-eval with the *nath-cult* and having many points in common.

The *dharma-cult* was a degraded form of Buddhism, and *nath-cult* was a compromise between *saivism* and *buddhism*. The followers of both the cults believed in '*niranjan*' and '*dharma*', though the *nath-cult* seems to have adhered more closely to *Siva*-worship, but both believed in miracles and in the supernatural powers of the siddhas. As a matter of discussion and research under which circumstances such an old tradition and philosophical cult, like the *nath-cult* has diminished. The *sakta-cult*, which was probably the principal element in the Hinduism of that day, was neither a spiritual nor an aesthetic influence in religion. Sri Chaitanya was born in such a condition, when the society was pressed upon from without spirituality and morality. The simple folk of the villages, among whom the practice of yoga and tantric culture had been current at that time.

It is admitted that during the declining power of Hinduism, the standards of morality had become low amongst the people of the *buddhist* and *nath* ascetics towards materialistic life. Tendencies to lead a sensuous life are manifest in popular literature of *Siva-cult*. It was the prevalent fashion in that age to be addicted to be a woman other than one's own wife for tantric practice. Amongst the Buddhist of the latter day, *Mahayana* and among their *bhikshus* and *bhikshunis*, the *sahaja-dharma* became associated within illicit love. The Hindu renaissance had just commenced among the lowest group of people of this province, but they were still pray to those vices which *tantricism* and perverted Buddhism had brought on during the decline of spiritual forces. The tantrics mainly strove with the help of human corpses, wine and women to attain a religious goal. The impetus which may alone lead to receive from Islam to grow of true faith. The Islam with its great tenets and appeal to personal *God* knocked at the gate of Bengal. They declared that one Great *God*, who was the supporter of the virtuous, was the supporter of the world. Their faith was very strong to change the Hindu mind. Chandi Das (a poet of Bengal) recognized that their province was in need of a savior, who would prove that the true spirited bliss sprang from faith, not from intellectual subtleties. Moral law and a sense of brotherhood were the concomitant forces of love which could alone bring the incomprehensible one within human realization.

At the time of Sri Chaitanya, religion was reduced to a mere form and there was no faith in men. The time was ripe for a reformer and savior. The offensive stagnation waited fervently for an undesirable movement. Sri Chaitanya's appearance and consequent behavior acted as the right dozes of cleaning medicine. So, Sri Chaitanya was a pioneer of Bengal Vaisnavism. It started a new phase of Lord *Krsna* worship in the form of *nama-sankirtana*, i.e. recitation or singing with devotion, the name and glory of the respective deity. The utterance of *Krsna-nama-sankirtana* was the real footprints for salvation. He hope, this could be bring certain religious changes in the medieval societies ultimately it led a popular movement. Whatever the political situation of Bengal had not crushed the intellectual class. Nadia's reputation was mainly due to a band of scholars, most of them were Sri Chaitanya's contemporaries. Sri Chaitanya apparently never tried to establish a new stamp of his individuality. He developed on the lines of his personal spiritual experience. It proved to be its greatest and most powerful asset. Bengal Vaisnavism, which is otherwise known as *Chaitanyaism* is a mixture of *emotionalism* and *spiritualism*.

Vrndavanadasa (the author of *Chaitanya Bhagavata*) is the foremost pioneer of the *bhakti*-school who for the first time came to establish that *Srikrsna* and Gauranga are identical, and the sole object of all living beings is to worship Him, and receive His blessings at any circumstances.

Many pandits of Navadvipa who were ill disposed towards Sri Chaitanya could recognize that these developments are only abnormal manifestations. They circulated the scandal that he had become mad. But a few true devotees in that region perceived in them the surge of divine emotion, and some recognized in him a divine incarnation. These incidents opened the eye of several people of Navadvipa, especially of the pandits who proud of their learning. They found that *bhakti* is not mere vapid emotional nonsense, but something solid, transparent and substantial that can be given by a great master to others at his will. This notion became still more confirmed when Sri Chaitanya demonstrated this power again by imparting *Krsna-bhakti* to a neighbor and friend Gadadhara and vainglorious ascetic Suklambar, by blessing them with a touch of his hand.

It is accurate to write of Sri Chaitanya in terms of social reform, or to credit him with a revolutionary social vision. It seems perfectly clear that he was not concerned with the reform of Hindu society. His sole interest was religion. It is only as his religious experience, that engendered by him among others, came into conflict with the Hindu social system that he can be called a social reformer. His social reform was only a by-product of his *bhakti*.

At that time, caste-division was predominant in the society. Sri Chaitanya's *bhakti* movement was of against this, which comes across and melts down the distinction between caste, creeds, and color. Here the word *caste* has its root in Persia. In India, when the Persians have started their trade, they called the social deviation as the *caste deviation*. In the *Gita*, it is also seen that the class division or deviation has occurred according to their ability and propensity. To remove this type of deviation from society, Sri Chaitanya has taken a strong step. He adopts this non-intellectual means or technique for the sake of the mass appeal without any discrimination.

Five hundred years ago, in Bengal, it was the system that persons who were born in the families of Brahmanas were accepted as *brahmanas*, and all those who took birth in other families—even the higher castes, namely the *ksatriyas* and *vaisyas*—were considered as *sudra*, non-brahmana. Sri Chaitanya did not accept this artificial principle, which was introduced in society by self-interested men. One of the examples is that, he stayed at the house of Chandrasekhara, a clerk. It is the tradition of the society at that time was, a *sanyasi*, is not supposed to reside in a *sudra's* house. So, the philosophy of Sri Chaitanya has discharged a formless society with love and compassion.

Sri Chaitanya did not consistently set himself against the caste system. He went far beyond the customs and ideas of his time in the direction of a brotherhood of *bhakti*. Sri Chaitanya repeatedly proclaimed his *bhakti* as being accessible to the lowest classes of Hindu society.

Sri Chaitanya had found the caste system eating the vitals of social fabric. He and his followers were determined to root out this 'evil' from the land. Nityananda was appointed by him to stay in Bengal with the sole charge of social reformation. According to Sri Chaitanya, a *chandala* should be held higher than brahmana if he has devotion for *God*. This is a well-known text of the *Naradiya Purana* also. Sri Chaitanya not only preached the equality of men but sometimes advocated a somewhat forward step in the practice of this doctrine. Sri Chaitanya never cares for caste; he is a sea of compassion and embraces Chandalas and other low-castes with passion. One of the friends of Sri Chaitanya, Sivananda says in a song that the high and low in the social scale are brought to the same level by Sri Chaitanya. Balaram Das repeats the same idea that "he weeps embracing the fallen, the destitute and the low".

From the historical interpretation, it is revealed that during the medieval period, what the legend says, the king Purusottama Deva performs the functions of a *chandala*. It is not that the function of sweeping the chariot was previously assigned to a *chandala* and the king became so liberal, so as to take over that function. The point here is that, the idea behind this legend is, there is no social station is higher or lower, is to be appreciated. And during the car festival by sweeping the thence chariots is the symbol of love and devotion to the Supreme *God*. Simultaneously, Sri Chaitanya's philosophy has been absorbed in Sri *Jagannathism* in the sense of *bhakti* or devotion.

Thc social consequences of Sri Chaitanya's religious experience came from the catholicity of his *bhakti*. He recognized no limits whatever to be set to this absorbing experience, and the participation of men in it. In short, it may be said that he had courage to preach a message of religious freedom, which made a place for all in its cult of loving devotion. Naturally, this gave his movement a tremendous appeal to the hearts of the common people.

Theoretical knowledge of love of *God* can be found in many places and in many scriptures, but what that love of Godhead actually is and how it is developed can be found in Vaisnava literatures. It is the unique and highest development of love of *God* that is given by Sri Chaitanya. By the mercy of the supreme personality of Godhead, he even an inexperienced boy with no educational culture can be saved from the ocean of nescience, which is full of various types of philosophical doctrines that are like dangerous aquatic animals.

It is a mistake to think of Sri Chaitanya as in any sense, the originator of Vaisnavism in Bengal. It is necessary to attempt a very brief sketch of the development of Vaisnavism. Since it shares the *Krsna-cult* and the fundamental theology of that cult with other sects of Vaisnavism, it is well to trace the rise of these ideas as a whole. The worshipper of *Visnu* can claim a long tradition for this, *God* is found in the *Vedas*, very early in this *Visnu* cult, the image worship of the temples, as opposed to the worship of sacrifice of the Vedic tradition. The distinctive feature of this widespread cult was the rise of *bhakti* as the heart of worship, an emotional service of love and devotion to *God*. The figures of *Rama* and *Krsna* early arise as incarnations of *Visnu*, and become supreme objects of devotion leading to the varied development of the sects. Parallel with this development, there arose the great Hindu philosophies—the *Vedanta*, the *Sankhya*, the *Yoga*—all having great influence. About the beginning of the Christian era, a notable point in the history is reached with the attempt on the part of some keen mind to combine these philosophies and appropriate them for the exaltation of Lord *Krsna* worship.

In the *Bhagavad Gita*, a remarkable work that identifies Lord *Krsna* with the eternal *Brahman* has retains his personal nature, and thus, forms a truly monotheistic faith. After the philosophies and epics, there arose the *Puranas*, which are important in Vaisnava literature. Of the great sects of Vaisnavism, the Sri Vaisnavas (Ramanuja Vaisnava) of the Tamil country are the most inclusive, forming their system on the whole of Vaisnavism and recognizing all the incarnations of *Visnu*. The other sects are devoted to particular incarnations, with the figure of Lord *Krsna*. In the *Bhagavata-purana*, there is a suggestion of a favorite *gopi* with whom Lord *Krsna* wonders and sports alone. From this time, the cult of *Radha-Krsna* developed. *Radha* occupying a position of very great importance. This cult spread eventually throughout the north and into the south.

History says Sri Chaitanya alone is solely responsible for introducing *Radha* concept to a much esteemed position, although other Vaisnava thinkers, like Madhva, Nimbarka exalted only Lord *Krsna* in front of the society. So, it can be said that Sri Chaitanya not only an originator of Vaisnavism, but also started a *neo-vaisnavite* movement by rendering a new interpretation to the faith. The doctrine of *bhakti* and adoration to *Radha-Krsna* cult shaped a new style to tackle the common mass. Sri Chaitanya's *neo-vaisnavite* movement was reincarnated him as *Sri Krsna Chaitanya* by the society. Because of his intense emotional influence, he easily touched the heart of the people of all castes and creeds.

Only the Sri Vaisnavas (the Visnu Svamins), who developed next had little to distinguish them from the Madhvas, except their worship of *Radha* in conjunction with Lord *Krsna*. A third group arose 11th to 13th century led by Nimbarka. He developed a middle position in this philosophical system called *bhedabheda*, a dualistic monism, by which the *God* and the Soul are conceived as at the same time one and yet distinct. His sect is important for its exaltation of *Radha* not simply as the chief of the *gopis*, but as the eternal consort of Lord *Krsna*, become incarnate with him in the Vrndavana scenes. But early in the 16th century, Vallabhacharya's philosophy and Sri Chaitanya's philosophy sprang up at about the same time. Vallabhacharya was much nearer to Sankara's monism in his philosophical position than is true of these other sects, but in his theology he seems to have followed Nimbarka's theory of *Radha and Krsna*.

The time and manner spread the *Radha-Krsna* cult into Bengal is very difficult to determine. There is no history of this process. Indeed, we are in the dark about the whole early history of the *Radha* story and how it spread across north India. It seems a reasonable supposition that the *name* appears and Her cult begins at Vrndavana sometime in the 11th century. The development of this cult in Bengal was colored by conditions more or less peculiar to this province. In Bengal, the concept of *Radha-Krsna* came into contact with *tantricism* in both Hindu and Buddhist guise. The Brahmachari School of the *sakta-cult* is the Hindu product, and the *sahajiya-cult* seems to have been its counterpart in the decaying Buddhism of the centuries previous to Sri Chaitanya's day. The *sakta-cult* of Hinduism was powerful and active at that time. Clear evidence of tantric influence upon Vaisnavism was found in the life of the important Bengali poet, named Chandi Das, who was born a full century before Sri Chaitanya. He was a *sakta*. As his best-known songs are in praise of *Radha and Krsna*. It is evident that he became a devotee of the *Radha-Krsna* cult and brought into it the *sahajiya* influence. Beyond the tantric contribution of Buddhism already treated, it is the more general absorption of Buddhist adherents and ideas into the new sect. This was more marked in Puri. In Odisha, where Buddhism continued longer than in Bengal. It was probably the prevailing religious influence among the common people until Sri Chaitanya's time. It seems clear that when the Vaisnava preachers, a generation after Sri Chaitanya, swept the countryside with their proselytizing, many of their adherents came out of Buddhism. These people evidently brought much of their old thought with them into the new fold. The principal Vaisnava poets of Odisha were still much under Buddhist influence. They became followers of Sri Chaitanya, when his movements swept, that are created much of the Vaisnava literature of Odisha, but their thought while cast in vaisnava forms, still retained much that was distinctively Buddhist.

Too much has been made of the debt of Vaisnavism to Buddhism. It is also a claim that most of the characteristic features of the Vaisnava sects were copied from Buddhism. These features have their roots in pre-buddhist Hindu practice, and derive from thence whatever may have been the process of development. It is said that Sri Chaitanya's movement received from buddhism, a distinct legacy, which it could well have done without. This consisted of the remnants of its monastic orders. The degraded *bhikshus* and *bhikshunis* of decayed Buddhism had no standing in the Hindu community, and their own moral condition was not such as to make them welcome in any orderly society. They were products of *tantricism* at its worst. They lived in promiscuity, and were looked upon as outcastes. Their religious origin and their utter lack of rooted social tradition made them peculiarly susceptible to absorption in a new religious movement; while to a new sect with full of propagandist zeal is considered as a body of detached and destitute religionists offered at once a temptation and an appeal.

There are many followers of Vaisnava cult at the time of Sri Chaitanya who does not accept the conclusions of the *sastras*, and therefore, they are considered to be *apa-sampradaya*, which means 'outside of the *sampradaya*'. Vaisnavas must not be disrespectful to anyone. Sri Chaitanya can give more than salvation due to his magnanimous character. But the word *hinarthadhika sadhakam* indicates that although by material estimation, *salvation* is of a quality superior to the inferior interests of religiosity, economic development and sense gratification, above *salvation*. There is the position of devotional service and transcendental love for the supreme personality of Godhead.

King Prataparudra Deva of suryavansi dynasty of Odisha was a great devotee of Sri Chaitanya. He was religious-minded, which is the one of the reasons for Sri Chaitanya to stay for a long time at Puri and another reason for his staying there is that though his ancestors lived at Jajpur of Odisha, which is found in the writings of Jayananda's *Chaitanya Mangala*, he wanted to settle there on sentimental ground. It was by the arrangement of Ramananda Raya and Sarvabhauma Bhattacharya that he (King Prataparudra Deva), was able to serve Sri Chaitanya. Such development of *Vaisnavism* in Odisha is evident from the insurrection of the said dynasty. The people of Odisha have taken him for granted that Sri Chaitanya had divinity like Lord Jagannath. It is also mentioned in the *Chaitanya Chandrodaya* nataka of Kavi Karnapura that Sri Chaitanya is *nara brahma* (human embodiment of Brahma) and Lord Jagannath is *daru brahma* (wooden embodiment of *Brahma*).

In the history, it is observed that Vaisnavism became a state religion of Odisha from the time of Chodaganga Deva of Ganga dynasty, and under the influence of Ramanuja, he adopts *Vaisnava-dharma* and for the result, he constructed the temple of Lord *Jagannath* and *Laksmi* at Puri. It is also mentioned that from that time onwards *Visnu-Laksmi* cult gained popularity in Odisha. It clearly shows that under the great impact of Vaisnavism, Lord *Jagannath* placed a high position in Oriya's mind.

Sri Rupa Gosvami recommends that an acharya should devise a means by which people may somehow or other come to *Krsna-consciousness.* First, they should become *Krsna-conscious*, and all the prescribed rules and regulations may later gradually be introduced. *Krsna-consciousness* movement is based on a solid philosophy of transcendental science. After understanding the *Bhagavata* philosophy, or the *Bhagavata-dharma*, they become fully spiritually conscious or *Krsna-conscious*, and their chanting and dancing is not material, but is on the spiritual platform. One cannot obtain *Krsna-bhakti*, or the devotional service of the lord by official execution of the Vedic rituals. In the next chapter, we have to discuss the further development of the concept of *bhakti* in brief.

2

Sri Chaitanya's Concept of Bhakti

The word *bhakti* is derived from the root *bhaj*, which means to share, to allot, to distribute, to divide, to assign, etc. *Bhakti* or devotion means supreme love for *God*. According to Tapasyananda, the conception of *bhakti* has played an important role in the religious history of India. It is not the exclusive legacy of any sect or religion; on the contrary, it forms the core of every theistic religion. It may be defined as an ardent and hopeful devotion to a particular deity in grateful recognition of aid received or promised. It often assumes the form of a passionate love of the deity, whether *God* or *Goddess*. Its marks are surrender of the self to the divine being and acts of devotion either in some sanctified place or in private life and thought.

Bhakti is deeply rooted in Indian tradition. *Moksa* or liberation can be attained by three ways, i.e. *karma*, *jnana*, and *bhakti*. The first important literary recognition of *bhakti-marga* as a true way of salvation was made in the famous *Bhagavad Gita*. The service of the senses through the senses is called *bhakti*.

The *bhakti* movement can be clearly divided into two distinct periods. The first was from the time of the *Gita* to 14th century, and the second from 14th century to 16th century. The first phase of the *bhakti* movement was only an individual sentiment, whereas the second phase was both emotional as well as spiritual.

In the *Chaitanya Bhagavata*, it is said that the roots of the *bhakti* movement, which Madhavendra Puri (guru of Isvar Puri) is said to have started in Bengal and which Chaitanya carried forward and definitely shaped, must be sought in such traditions as originated from Sridhara's great commentary on the *Bhagavata* which was accepted with much veneration by the Vaisnavas. The *Bhagavata* preaches the cult of unmotivated devotion *(ahetuki bhakti*) to *God*. That is the highest religion of man from which selflessness and uninterrupted devotion to *God* arises, which fills the soul with bliss. In this sense, *bhakti* is described as "*sa paranuraktir Isvare*" in the *Sandilya Bhakti Sutra*. Absolute devotion or utter adoration is the keynote of this emotion. *Bhakti* is the only and the primary sentiment. It is supernatural. There is no I-ness of self in this feeling. Devotion as a method to attain supreme bliss has a rival in the method of knowledge, because knowledge uncovers the true nature of any object, while devotion establishes most intimate relationship with even the most attainable one. Devotion leads to Him, devotion uncovers Him. According to Narada, *bhakti* comprises three elements: it is the highest love for *God*, a surrender of actions to Him, and agony when He is forgotten. Thus, it can be said that devotion can be described as a bridge between the devotee and *God*. It is firmed rooted in faith and fervor. He holds that that devotion is higher than action, higher than knowledge and higher than concentration of mind. It is higher than any other means of salvation, because it is its own reward. Knowledge and action are motivated by egoism and pride. So, they cannot excite *God's* compassion.

There was no scope for devotion or *bhakti* as a principal sentiment. The claim of *bhakti* as a full-fledged emotion was forwarded. Since *bhakti* is conceived as a *rasa*, it is essentially of the nature of a subjective emotion. There is no such sentiment that developed cannot be transformed into an emotion. One objection of the critics is that *bhakti*, being of fluctuating disposition, cannot be equal to the status of *asthayibhava*. *Asthayibhava* is the sentiment, which should be self-sufficient enough to be transformed into an emotion. The devotion is a many-splendored sentiment. It cannot be included within the jurisdiction of *santa*, because in *santa*, total disinterest is the primary element, while in devotion, unselfish love predominates.

Bhakti or devotion is free from desire and is of the nature of exhibition of all desires, by which, is meant not the extinction of all desires, but the consecration of all desires and action to *God*. It is almost impossible to suppress all desires and passions. We can only divert their course. Naturally, they are directed towards *God*. We should dedicate all our actions to Him and cherish all our passions, desire, anger, egoism, and the like only for Him. *Bhakti* is a surging emotion which chokes the speech, makes the tears flow and the hair thrill with pleasurable excitement, and often leads to hysterical laughing and weeping by turns, to sudden fainting fits, and to long trances of unconsciousness.

It is said in the *Chaitanya Bhagavata* that a life of devotion is not necessarily a life of inaction. That is real action, which pleases *God*. In other words, the actions those are done for the pleasure of *God* without any desire for their fruits. The complete surrender of the soul to *God* is needed for reaching the ultimate goal. We should purge ourselves of egoism for this.

Bhakti is exemplified in the life of Sri Chaitanya and is recorded by the Navadvipa devotees. The enthusiastic physical and emotional appeal was not only congenial to the essentially emotional faith, but it was also utilized effectively for spreading the contagion of *bhakti*. A *bhakta* will serve

a human being. The knot of egoism will be broken, doubts will disappear, and the results of past actions wither away. *Bhakti* is particularly efficacious for the householders who are tried to their worldly affairs. For such people, the only way to salvation is to hear Lord *Krsna*'s *Lila-katha-rasa*.

Desire never ends. Satisfaction of one begets another. So, Lord *Krsna* leads a man away from all desires to the asylum of His lotus like feet, just as a mother takes a piece of clay out of her child's mouth and gives him a piece of candy. According to Jiva Gosvami, *bhakti* is the highest form of human activity. It is eternal. It is capable of melting (the results of) *karma* as fire melts gold. The similar example has given also in the *Srimad Bhagavad Gita* that *jnana* melts *karma*. In this sense, Vaisnava's thought is different from the *Bhagavad Gita*. *Bhakti* is universal for them. Even if a great sinner pays undivided and exclusive devotion to Lord *Krsna*. He should be considered to be a Saint, and a real devotee even if immersed in worldly affairs, is not over whelmed. *Bhakti* is not only the supreme virtue; it is also the universal purifier. *Karmas* are *saguna* whereas *bhakti* is *nirguna*. It is self-revealing, and is extremely blissful. Sins are removed by listening to the recital of His name.

Bhakti is the means (*sadhana*) as well as end (*sadhya*). Though *bhakti* destroys all obstacles, and results in *preman*, one should not on its strength desire for something else. *Bhakti* can be alloyed with three types of desires, which are called as *sakama*, *kaivalya-kama*, and *bhakti-matra-kama*.

Sa-kama-bhakti is usually mixed with *karman*, which in the present instance means *dharma*, i.e. the performance of vedic rites in order to get some desirable objects, like a son, empire, wealth, etc. *kaivalya-kama-bhakti* is sometimes alloyed with *karman* and sometimes with *jnana*, or with both. *Jnana* here means visualization of identity with the *Bhagavata*. Hence, such *bhakti* leads to *moksa*. When the goal is pure *bhakti* (it may be mixed with *karman*), is called as *bhakti-matra-kama*.

Though the Gosvamins (Rupa and Sanatana) have extolled the way of *bhakti*, they have not denied the efficacy of other ways of devotion. In fact, Jiva Gosvami's attempt was not to denounce *karma* and *jnana* as means of salvation, but to prove the superiority of *bhakti* over them.

'One must engage his tongue in the service of the holy name'—'*Krsna consciousness movement*' is based on this principle. One cannot obtain *Krsna-bhakti* or the devotional service of the Lord by official execution of the Vedic rituals. While executing devotional service, one must be naturally inclined to serve Lord *Krsna* in one of these transcendental relationships. That is the actual success of life. It is said in the *Chaitanya Charitamrta* that the only supreme master is Lord *Krsna*, and all others, both *Visnu-tattva* and *jiva-tattva* engage in the service of the lord. In this sense, *Krsna consciousness movement* is not stereotyped or stagnant. In the *Bhakti Sandarbha*, Jiva Gosvami has stated that those who are actually very serious about devotional service do not differentiate between the *Form of the Lord* made of clay, metal, stone or wood, and the *Original form of the Lord*.

The Lord is manifested to a pure devotee from within and without. This is one of the mysteries of the devotional relationship in which a devotee and the Lord are bound by a tie of spontaneous love. A pure devotee knows that when he chants the transcendental name *Krsna*, *Srikrsna* is presented as transcendental sound. He, therefore, chants with full respect and veneration. A devotee does not see anything except in its relationship with Lord *Krsna*, and his realization is the most perfect of all. The absolute conception of a pure devotee includes all others.

One who engages in the spiritual activities of unalloyed devotional service (*avyabhicharini bhakti*) is immediately elevated to the transcendental platform, and he is to be considered as *Brahma-bhakta*, which indicates that he is no longer in the material world but in the spiritual world.

The *gopis* of Vraja came out to meet Lord *Krsna* in the dead of night when they heard the sounds of Lord *Krsna's* flute. By leaving home in that way, the *gopis* have transgressed the Vedic regulations of household life. This indicates that when natural feelings of love for Lord *Krsna* become fully manifest, a devotee can neglect conventional social rules and regulations. In the material world, we are situated in designative positions only, but pure devotional service begins when one is freed from all designations. When love for Lord *Krsna* is awakened, then the designative positions are overcome. There is a great increase of mellow in the unwedded conjugal mood. Such love is found nowhere but in Vraja.

According to the *Chaitanya Charitamrta*, *Radha* and *Krsna* are one and the same, but they have assumed two bodies. *Srimati Radhika* is the transformation of Lord *Krsna's* love. She is His internal energy called *hladini*. *Hladini* is the personal manifestation of the blissfulness of the supreme personality of Godhead. *Hladini* is His aspect of bliss; *sandhini*, of eternal existence; and *samvit*, of cognizance, which is also accepted as knowledge. The essence of the *samvit* potency is knowledge that the supreme personality of Godhead is Lord *Krsna*. All other kinds of knowledge, such as the knowledge of *Brahman*, are its components. The essence of the *hladini* potency to love of *God* is *bhava* (emotion), and the ultimate development of *bhava* is *mahabhava*. *Sri Radha* Thakurani is the embodiment of *mahabhava*. *Radha* is the one who gives pleasure to *Krsna*, and she is also the enchantress of Lord *Krsna*. She is the Be-all and End-all of Lord *Krsna*, and the crest jewel of all His consorts. The divine love between *Radha* and *Krsna* is not an ordinary human affair; it is fully transcendental. In order to understand *Radha* and *Krsna*, worship Them and engage in Their loving service.

The love of the *gopis* is called *sudha-bhava*. It is pure and spotless. It is not at any time lust. The *gopis* saw their beloved Lord *Krsna* at Kurukshetra after a long separation. They secured and embraced Him in their hearts through their eyes, and they attained a joy so intense that not even perfect yogis can attain it. The yogis cursed the creator for creating eyelids that interfered with their vision. Anyone who thinks that Lord *Krsna* is a product of material energy, as explained by Sadananda Yogindra, should immediately is understood to be insane, for his knowledge has been stolen by the illusory energy. In the *Hari-bhakti-vilasa*, Sri Sanatana Gosvami gives definite instructions that by proper initiation by a bona fide spiritual master one can immediately become a Brahmana. In this connection, he says, as all metal is turned to gold when mixed with mercury in an alchemical process, so one who is properly trained and initiated by a bona fide spiritual master immediately becomes a Brahmana.

Sri Chaitanya School views *bhakti* as an inherent quality of *Bhagavan* and also believes that an atom of *bhakti* remains present in the *jiva* in a potential manner, although it is in an unmanifested form. The manifestation of *bhakti* takes place only when the jiva realizes his own nature; it becomes possible only when he develops faith in Lord *Krsna*.

Classification of Bhakti

Bhakti is classified in several ways. The classification is based on the quality involved in it, on the intention of the devotee, on the relation between the devotee and *God*, etc. There are three categories of devotion based on quality, namely one, which is dominated by purity, the other, which is dominated by passion and the third, which is dominated by inertia. *Bhakti* can also be categorized on the basis of the intention of the devotee, such as the *arta*, i.e. he who prays

God to remove his calamity; *artharthi*, i.e. he who prays *God* for some material gain such as wealth, progeny, success, etc.; and *jijnasu*, i.e. he who prays *God* in order to have knowledge of the ultimate reality and he who is a realized soul and still continues to meditate upon *God* because it becomes his inner nature.

The third classification is *para bhakti* and *apara bhakti*. *Para-bhakti* is considered to be superior to the *apara-bhakti*. In the latter kind of devotion a devotee considers himself as separate from *God* yearning for His vision. From this stage when he goes further on the spiritual path he becomes one with *God*. Still he is fond of the sweetness of the ambrosia, which he relishes when he remembers *God*. Even after experiencing the union with *God*, he desires to consider himself separate from him to continue with the enjoyment of the nectar of the bliss, which is the outcome of his devotion towards Lord. So he imagines himself as separate from *God*, even though he is fully aware of the unity. This is the stage of *para-bhakti*, the Supreme devotion which is known as *jnanottara-bhakti*-post knowledge devotion, which is the ultimate goal of the endeavor of a devotee. *God* cares only for devotion. There is nothing small or great to Him. He is considered only with the spirit in which it is offered.

The *Bhagavata* glorifies the *bhakti-yoga*, and classified it into three major types according to the three *gunas*, *sattva*, *rajas*, and *tamas*. Each is again subdivided into three minor types according to the specific type of inclinations on the part of the devotee. Apart from this, it also emphasizes upon the classical *navadha-bhakti* (*nirguna* or *niskama-bhakti*), which represents the highest type. This is marked by a desire less state of mind, which is directed towards *Bhagavan*. Such a direction of the mind to *Bhagavan* is described as natural (*svabhavika*), not vitiated by any partisan outlook (*avyavahita*), selfless (*ahetuki*) and is not interrupted by any other thought. The *Bhagavata*, thus, views devotion as an act of dedication to *God* and objectively, the duty of a man lie in the performance of all his actions in complete dedication to *God*.

According to Jiva Gosvami, though *bhakti* is being the central theme, its efficacies remain universal in nature. So, *bhakti* is said to be *sarva-kamaprada*, *asubha-harini*, *sarva-vighna-nasini*, *sarva-bhaya-klesa-nasini*, *papa-harini* and so on and so forth.

According to Rupa Gosvami, *bhakti* is of three types, namely *sadhana bhakti*, *bhava bhakti*, and *prema bhakti*. *Sadhana-bhakti* is realized by senses and it awakens the inward emotion (*bhava*). *Sadhana-bhakti* is sub-classified into two types, namely *vaidhi-bhakti* (devotion according to the injunctions of the scriptures) and *raganuga-bhakti* (spontaneous devotion). *Raganuga-bhakti* presupposes *ragatmika-bhakti* (devotion with attachment to the Lord) and follows the latter. *Ragatmika-bhakti* is also of two kinds, namely *prema-rupa-bhakti* (devotion to the Lord for winning His love) and *sambandha-rupa-bhakti* (devotion to the Lord with some relation with Him). Similarly, *raganuga-bhakti* has also the similar varieties. When attachment to the Lord softens the heart, it is called *bhava-bhakti*. It consists of mainly five *bhavas* (emotions), namely *santa* (quietism), *dasya* (servitude), *sakhya* (friendship), *vatsalya* (parental affection), and *madhura* (sweet sentiment of a lover for the beloved). When *bhava-bhakti* softens the heart further and creates a sense of intense feeling for making *God* one's own beloved, *bhakti* is being possessed of *prema* (divine love). It may be the result of *vaidhi-bhakti*, *raganuga-bhakti* or the benediction of Lord *Krsna*. *Prema* again is of two kinds. In the first, the devotee is conscious of the majesty and grandeur of the Lord *(aisvarya)*, while in the other, the love is free from such inhibiting knowledge and is, called *kevala prema* (pure love). *Prema* unfolds itself into *sneha*, *mana*, *pranaya*, *raga*, *anuraga*, *bhava*, and *mahabhava*. *Prema* is further divided into *vipralambha* (separation), and *sambhoga* (union).

Sri Rupa Gosvami has prescribed 64 rites for a devotee for the attainment of *sadhana bhakti*. A similar number has also been recorded by Krsnadasa Kaviraja considering them as *angas* or elements of *sadhana-bhakti*. At a later stage, Jiva Gosvami reduced the number to eleven that are *saranapatti*, *guru seva*, *sravana*, *kirtana*, *smarana*, *padasevana*, *archana*, *vandana*, *dasya*, *sakhya*, and *atmanivedana*.

Saranapatti consists in resorting to *Bhagavan* as the only and the ultimate refuge (*ananya-gati*). This act of refuge becomes possible when one becomes aware of the dreadful consequences of worldly life. Having no other alternative, he takes refuge in *God* as the only protector who can help him to overcome sufferings.

In *guru-seva* or devotion to the *guru*, Jiva Gosvami says, the *guru* being the mediator between the devotee and his *Bhagavan*, he must be accorded a pre-eminent position; consequently, devotion to guru should be considered as more vital than the same to Lord *Krsna*.

Sravana denotes the act of listening to the details of the name, form, qualities and sports of Lord *Krsna*. So far as the efficacy of the name of Lord *Krsna* is concerned, it is mentioned in the *Bhagavata* that by listening to His name, even a *chandala* becomes transformed into a devotee while being free from all worldly attachments. Although there are no definite rules as to whether one should listen to one or more of these different kinds of accounts, yet Jiva Gosvami considers listening to the *Bhagavata* as the best type of *sravana*.

Kirtana is complementary to *sravana* and remains as the most important and the most effective of all the devotional practices. Sri Chaitanya himself gives supreme importance to *kirtana* stating that it remains the only means of *God*-realization in the age of Kali.

Smarana indicates mental investigation or inquiry into the name, qualities, and sports of Lord *Krsna* and His *parikaras* (attendants). In the *Bhagavata*, *smarana*, in general, is described as complete surrendering of the mind to Lord *Krsna* while remaining detached from the worldly objects. Practically speaking, *smarana* means everlasting meditation of Lord *Krsna*, which remains uninterrupted by any other thought. For the Gaudiyas, there are five stages of *smarana,* namely *smarana samanya*, representing a continuous flow of thought round the object of meditation; *dharana* or fixing the mind on the object of thought by withdrawing from other objects; *dhyana* meaning an undisturbed concentration on the name, form, qualities, and sports of Lord *Krsna*; *dhrubanusmrti*, the uninterrupted flow of the mind towards the goal like a stream of nectar; and lastly, *samadhi*, connoting complete self-absorption on the object and the exclusive appearance of the object of thought in the mind.

Pada-sevana, which includes seeing, touching and going round (*parikrama*) the image; it also includes following the procession of the image of the *God*, bathing in the holy rivers, etc.

In *archana*, one is entitled to perform ritualistic worship only if he is initiated from the *guru*. Once a devotee adopts *archana* as a means, he must follow certain rules and regulations as enjoined in the Vaisnava scriptures very strictly.

Vandana or the act of homage includes salutation by prostrating at full length like a log of wood.

Dasya is the feeling of servitude to Lord *Krsna*. Besides actual services, it consists of such feelings that, 'I am the servant of my Lord'. Such a feeling is said to be present in all the devotional practices. All devotional practices attain superiority on account of such relations.

Sakhya, like *dasya* also follows the very nature of the relations between *jiva* and *Bhagavan*. It is the feeling of fellowship with the Lord.

Atma-nivedana means complete dedication of the self. It is complete self-surrender, where the devotee feels that his body, mind, soul and the senses are all intended for the service of Lord *Krsna*.

Bhava Bhakti

Sri Rupa Gosvami defines, when the generic character of *bhakti* strongly supported by various forms of taste, softens the heart, the reasoning faculty and the whole mental quantum, it is called *bhava-bhakti*. It is said in the tantra that the first stage of *prema* is *bhava*. There is partial manifestation of tears, horripilation, paleness, and other *sattvika-bhavas* in *bhava-bhakti*. The *bhava* consists of the longing for union with the Lord and the intense desire for His benediction and friendship. Sri Rupa Gosvami is of the view that this *bhava* appears in the heart of rare and extraordinary fortunate devotees. The causes of its appearance are either the intense ardor for spiritual practices or the spontaneous benediction of Lord *Krsna* and His devotees. The *bhava-bhakti* is full of warmth of love. By annoying the devotees of the Lord, *bhava* may disappear completely. So, the devotee should guard himself from committing any offence against the devotees of the Lord.

In the *Bhakti Rasamrta Sindhu*, it is described that in the stage of *bhava*, there are nine symptoms become manifest. These are:

1. *Ksanti*—even though a cause for agitation may be present, the devotees learnt remains unagitated.
2. *Avyartha-kalatva*—a devotee does not waste time in activities that are not directed towards the cultivation of *bhakti*.

3. *Virakti*—detachment from the objects of sense-enjoyment.
4. *Mana-sunyata*—pridelessness.
5. *Asa-bandha*—a firm hope of attaining *Bhagavan.*
6. *Utkantha*—intense longing for the Lord.
7. *Nama-gane sada-ruchi*—ever relishing a strong taste to chant the holy name.
8. *Asaktis tad-gunakhyane*—attachment for hearing and chanting the qualities of *Bhagavan.*
9. *Pritis tad-vasati-sthale*—love for the places where the Lord enacted His transcendental pastimes.

When the heart becomes melted by *ruchi*, then what was previously *sadhana-bhakti* is called *bhava-bhakti.* The primary characteristic of *bhava* is that it is a phenomenon constituted entirely of *visuddha-tattva. Visuddha-tattva* is the self-revealing agency of the internal potency (*chit-sakti*), comprised of *hladini*, *sandhini*, and *samvit*, through which the Lord and His associates are revealed to the devotees. This means that *bhava* is completely beyond the influence of material nature, and as such it is compared to a ray of the sun of *prema-bhakti.*

Bhava Bhakti and Bhakti Rasa

Bhava is a feeling and it is the function of the heart. In other words, when *anuraga* reaches a special state of intensity, it is known as *bhava. Rasa* means relish or that which is tasted or relished. If any sentiment combined with other sentiments or feelings becomes more delicious and creates an ineffable wonderfulness of bliss in the heart, it is said to be transformed into *rasa.* If the senses, the external and the internal, are concentrated in tasting the wonderful bliss is called *rasa.* When *rati*, the initial stages of *priti*, mixes with the four *vibhavas*—*vibhava*, *anubhava*, *sattvika-bhava*, and *vyabhichari-bhava*. It is transformed into the relishable experience known as *bhakti-rasa*.

Although *bhakti-rasa* is one, yet it manifests itself in various forms. According to Rupa Gosvami, there are five primary and seven secondary *bhakti-rasas*. The five primary *bhakti-rasas* are *santa-rasa*, *priti-bhakti-rasa* (or *dasya-rasa*), *preyo-bhakti-rasa* (or *sakhya-rasa*), *vatsalya-rasa*, and *madhurya-rasa*.

Santa Rasa

It usually leads to self-realisation, but it lacks in depth. The devotees of *santa-rasa* have exclusive devotion to Lord *Krsna* and their true self. The *santa bhakta* is calm, peaceful, and gentle. In *santa rasa*, there is neither happiness, nor misery, nor envy, nor jealousy. All men are equal. Such a devotee understands the nature of Lord *Krsna* but he cannot enjoy His love as of a beloved.

Priti Bhakti Rasa or Dasya Rasa

According to Sridhara Svami, *dasya-rasa* is the best of all the *rasas* and according to Sudeva, it is the foundation of love. In *dasya-rasa*, a devotee considers himself as servant of the Lord. In this *rasa*, there is love and the feeling of inferiority combined, because the Lord is treated as the *Supreme Task Master*.

Preyo Bhakti Rasa or Sakhya Rasa

Sakhya-rasa consists of mainly two elements of *dasya-rasa*, namely concentration on Lord *Krsna* and loving service and in addition to these two, it possesses one more element, i.e. trust. While a loving servant has deep regards for his master, a loving friend has a sense of equality, trust and confidence in his compeer. There is neither vanity nor sense of superiority in loving friendship. The Lord is fond of the *sakhya-rasa* as He is fond of His friends.

Vatsalya Bhakti Rasa or Vatsalya Rasa

The parental affection includes the three elements of *sakhya-rasa* and in addition, it consists of affection stronger than that of the friend. In such affection, the parents take child *Srikrsna* as their protege and themselves as His protectors. The Lord also responds to the parental call of His own devotees.

Madhurya Bhakti Rasa

Sri Chaitanya said that the divine love is called as *madhurya-rasa*. All the above *rasas* and in addition, the desire of placing the whole body at the service of the Lord. Thus, the *madhurya-rasa* consists of all the possible feelings mentioned in the above *rasas* and still more. The divine love is, therefore, the sweetest thing possible. In *madhurya-rasa*, a devotee feels himself as a woman in spirit, even though he may be a man in body. It is, therefore, natural to women. But even man adopts the temperament of a woman, viz. having entire dependence on the Lord and on love, mercy, tenderness, etc.

Prema Bhakti

Prema (love) is the deep affection for the Lord solidified into passion for Him. Once the real passion for the Lord appears in the heart, it never disappears. Sri Rupa Gosvami defines, when the *bhava* deepens to the maximum, it softens the heart completely and develops into the exceeding feeling for Lord *Krsna* as devotees' own. Thus, when the devotee is deeply attached to Lord *Krsna*, the wise designate it as *prema*. *Mamata* is the primary characteristic of *prema*. When an intimate relationship is there, then so many beautiful pastimes will also be there without these things, there is no feeling of *prema*. *Prema-bhakti* is said to have originated from two sources—one from *bhava-bhakti*, and the other by the special grace of the Lord. *Prema-bhakti* is of two types—one associated with the knowledge of greatness and majesty of the Lord and the other is *kevala prema*, which is one-pointed and all beauteous. Pure love is caused by knowledge of the all-beauteous form of Lord *Krsna*, i.e. *madhurya* only. The practice of *bhakti* calls us to draw back our love from the transient objects and creatures, which are the cause of misery and sorrow and concentrate our love in the Lord, our Creator and Source of all things. Thus, *bhakti* or *prema* elevates and culminates in a perpetual communion of the soul with God.

Prema has various stages of development according to the degree of intensity, viz. *prema*, *sneha*, *mana*, *pranaya*, *raga*, *anuraga*, *bhava*, *mahabhava*, etc.

Prema is the indissoluble bond of feeling that binds the soul with the Lord through all adverse circumstances.

Sneha is the end product of *prema* when the heart melts in love. It is of two types—in the former, the sentiment, viz. 'I am of the beloved' (*tadiyata*), and in the latter, the feeling, 'the beloved is mine' (*madiyata*), are the uppermost.

Mana is the highest manifestation of *sneha*, which can contain in it even the lack of generous response to Lord *Krsna*. In season or out of season, both the lover and the beloved become so very sensitive, often there arises anger and arrogance between them, but both intensify their love rather than lessen it as quarrels.

Pranaya is the product of *mana*. It gives way to unreserved confidence in Lord *Krsna's* love.

Raga is the final development of *pranaya* when to be really happy is to be smitten by the acute pangs of love. In this stage, the cause of great sorrow becomes the cause of great bliss.

Anuraga is the stage of love when it attracts to itself a sensation of unceasing novelty, a constant feeling of something not known before, always fresh and always new.

what Sri Chaitanya has to say about these concepts. And to show how they are distinctive of Sri Chaitanya. Of course, Sri Chaitanya is set to be composed *Siksastaka*, this is not about the philosophical topics, this is concerned about the spiritual education. We shall place our findings under the head of *metaphysics* and *epistemology*.

Metaphysics

The philosophical position of the Vaisnava Schools is a kind of concrete *absolutism* in which the personal absolute holds the totality of existence. According to Sri Chaitanya, the personal absolute enfolds the *nirvisesa* or formless, attributeless *Brahman*. Its nature is endlessly qualified and perfect. But the concept of the absolute as merely *nirvisesa* of Sankara which is beyond thought and speech is dismissed by him as meaningless. He says that such an absolute cannot be made the subject of an intelligible proposition. Any intelligible proposition about it would cancel the concept itself. Even to say that *Brahman* is inexpressible or unthinkable is to say or think something about it. In the *Kenopanisad,* it is said that "He who is not expressed by speech and by whom people here worship". When *Brahman* is said to be *asabdam* or ineffable, it does not mean that it cannot be expressed at all; but it cannot be completely expressed by words. If *Brahman* was completely beyond thought and speech, will have no meaning. In the *Sruti* text, it is said that *Brahman* is the subject of thought and speech. Being infinite and unbounded, *Brahman* cannot be cut in language.

But according to the Advaitins, *Brahman* is a pure existence, consciousness, and bliss etc. It is above the application of all kinds of difference, whether appears between things of the same category *(svajatiya)* or which appears between things of different categories (*vijatiya*) or which manifests itself in one and the same thing (*svagata*), either between its essence and form or between its component parts.

Sri Jiva Gosvami says that *nirvisesa Brahman* cannot be proved, because the object of proof is always *savisesa.* All objects of proof, according to the Advaitins, are perishable. In their absence of proof, the *nirvisesa* is unreal like the horns of a hare. Nor can it be accepted on the authority of the scriptures, because the scriptures depend on various forms of speech, which do not apply to it.

The *Brhadaranyaka Upanisad* describes *Brahman* as both conscious and bliss. In response, Jiva Gosvami explained about the words by saying consciousness is the negation of unconsciousness and bliss is the negation of unhappiness. Again bliss and consciousness are taken to refer to *vidya* (knowledge) as the negation of both unconsciousness and unhappiness, and though *vidya* is not independent of *Brahman*, it is an integral part of *Brahman-consciousness.* Knowledge as well as bliss is the functions of mind energized by its relation to *Brahman*; *Brahman* is not characterized by them but they are due to it.

In the *Chandogya Upanisad*, *Brahman* is not only qualified, but qualified in endless ways. The *Brahma Samhita* also describes *Brahman* as having a concrete form, made of *sat*, *chit* and *ananda.* But according to Sri Chaitanya, Sankara's view of unqualified *Brahman* is based mainly on indirect meaning. His exclusive emphasis on unqualified *Brahman* makes Him conceal the real and direct meaning of the *Sutras*, which describe *Brahman* as *savisesa* or qualified. The indirect meaning of words is justified only where the direct meaning does not make any sense.

Sri Jiva Gosvami's attempt to resolve the contradiction is more realistic. He relies upon the *Sastra*s for the real meaning of the words *savisesa* and *nirvisesa* by which *Brahman* is described as both qualified and unqualified. He quotes a sloka from the *Padma-Purana* to show that the word *nirvisesa* is used to deny all *prakrta* or worldly qualities of *Brahman* and not to deny qualities as such. If it were used to deny qualities as such it would not be possible to attribute to *Brahman*, the qualities of *nityatva* (eternity) and *vibhutva* (all-pervasiveness), which are accepted by the Advaitins themselves. Sri Chaitanya says that the difference between the qualified and the unqualified forms of *Brahman* is due to the difference between its *svarupa-laksana* (intrinsic nature) and *tatastha-laksana* (extrinsic nature), while the *svarupa-laksana* is the intrinsic nature of a thing; *tatastha-laksana* is the way it functions.

Sri Chaitanya's philosophy is called as *achintya bhedabheda*. His concept of *achintya* is different from Sankara's concept of *anirvachaniya*. Because Sankara's category of *anirvachaniya* is applicable to *maya* and its products, which can neither be described as real nor as unreal; it does not apply to *Brahman*, who is described as real. But Sri Chaitanya's category of '*achintya*' applies to the relation between *sakti* and *saktiman*, irrespective of the consideration whether it pertains to things in the phenomenal world or the transcendental world. It applies to *Brahman,* His associates and abodes as much as it applies to the *jivas* and the objects of the physical world. *Anirvachaniya* is a negative concept where as *achintya* is a positive concept. *Anirvachaniya* signifies the coming together of the opposite concepts of reality and unreality which cancel each other to produce illusion. *Achintya* signifies the tie of the opposite concepts of difference and non-difference leading to a higher and a complete unity. *Achintya* should also be distinguished from the category of *avaktavyam* (indescribable) of the Jaina philosophy.

Sri Jiva Gosvami has expounded the doctrine of *achintya-bhedabheda* in the context of the problem of relation between *God* and the *World*, and not in the context of the problem of relation between objects and their powers in general. The concept of *achintya* is found in numerous *Sruti* texts. The *Mandukya Upanisad*, *Kaivalya Upanisad*, and

Subala Upanisad describe *Brahman* as *achintya*. The *Gita* also describes Him as *achintya-rupa*. The scriptures describe *Brahman* as 'the greatest of the great' and 'the smallest of the small' as 'one who moves and yet moves not', as 'one who is far as well as near', 'immanent as well as transcendent', etc.

According to both Sankara and Sri Chaitanya, the absolute is devoid of all kinds of difference whether external or internal. But while Sankara says, the absolute is incapable of manifesting Himself in different forms without losing His oneness; Sri Chaitanya says that the absolute possesses the inconceivable power of doing so. Although He is one and indivisible, He has innumerable forms and manifests Himself in infinite ways to the devotees according to their different capacities and the different means of realization adopted by them. Thus, unlike Sankara and the other teachers of Vaisnavism, Sri Chaitanya does not stick exclusively to any one grade of realization of the absolute.

Sri Chaitanya says that the absolute *Bhagavan* is identified with the supreme personality of Lord *Krsna*, who is the source of all incarnations, the ultimate ground of all that exists, and in whom are centered infinite powers and infinite *rasa*s or modes of divine bliss. All the scriptures, explicitly or implicitly, speak of Lord *Krsna* as the ultimate reality. The *Srutis* describe the absolute as *nirvisesa* or unqualified, they do not deny its form and attributes. The body of the absolute and everything that pertains to Him is essentially transcendental or *aprakrta*. The existence of Lord *Krsna* rests on *suddha-sattva*, which is the essence of His *sandhini-sakti* or the divine Energy or pure existence. Everything in the phenomenal world is the manifestation of *misra-sattva*, which is qualified by *maya-sakti*.

Jiva Gosvami says that *paramatman* is a step higher than *Brahman* in the hierarchy of manifestations of the absolute personality of Lord *Krsna*. *Brahman* is the basic reality underlying all concrete formations. *Brahman* implies an absolutely undifferentiated and unqualified state of Lord *Krsna*. But He implies a differentiated and qualified state. *Paramatman* is *Bhagavan* or Lord *Krsna* in relation to *jiva* and *prakrti*. He creates the world and enters into it in the form of His partial manifested *Visnu*. *Paramatman* is no other than *Visnu* in His perfection, pervading and sustaining the entire universe. Sri Chaitanya says that Lord *Krsna*, *Bhagavan* has infinite *saktis* or energies, but most important of these are *chit-sakti*, *maya-sakti*, and *jiva-sakti*. They are not accidental but inherent in the nature of *Bhagavan*. *Maya* is a material manifestation, who serves *Bhagavan*.

The Vaisnava religions are based on a dynamic conception of reality. But the concept of *sakti* in Bengal Vaisnavism introduces a new and deeper rooted dynamism. Since the *saktis*, according to Bengal Vaisnavism, are related either externally or internally to *Bhagavan*. *Bhagavan* is essentially creative. His creative activity relating itself to two different planes—the cosmic reality and the Supra-cosmic reality, the order of nature and values, and the order of spirits. The former is the stirring of the external or *bahiranga-sakti*, which gives rise to the cycle order of creation and destruction. The latter is the stirring of the internal or *antaranga-sakti*, which manifests the eternal *lila* of Lord *Krsna*, *Bhagavan*. The eternal *lila* is the movement of the absolute spirit within itself. It precedes the order of values in transcendental beauty and sublimity of spiritual love, in beatitude and in the grace of movement.

Sankara's *nirvisesa Brahman* is the lowest manifestation of *svarupa-sakti*, and Lord *Krsna* is its highest manifestation. Lord *Krsna* is identical with *Bhagavan*. *Para-brahman* or the highest *Brahman* has infinite forms. Each is related to it as part is related to the whole. But since *para-brahman* has no internal difference, the part is not like a piece of stone chopped off from the whole. The part is actually the whole, the same all-powerful, all knowing and all-pervading being. Still, it is called a part; the *svarupa-sakti* of *para-brahman* is not fully manifested in it.

Both Sankara and Sri Chaitanya believe in *satkarya-vada* of the theory of causation, according to which, the cause and the effect are identical and the effect exists implicitly in the cause prior to its production. But according to Sri Chaitanya, the effect is real, what Sankara said it as illusory. According to him, the material cause and the effect are identical; the effect cannot be substantially different from the cause. The world being an effect of the *maya-sakti* of *Brahman* cannot be substantially different from the *maya-sakti*. Existence is an essential attribute of *maya-sakti*. It must be an essential attribute of the world. In other words, the world cannot be illusory. The theory that the world is illusory violates the theory of identity of cause and effect, which Sankara himself upholds.

Sri Chaitanya's *parinama-vada*, as applied to the problem of creation differs in an important respect from *parinama-vada* in the ordinary sense. In the ordinary sense, it means the modification of the material cause from which the world is produced. In Sankhya, it means the modification of *Prakrti* while in the *visistadvaita* of Ramanuja, it means the modification of the matter in *Brahman*, and therefore of *Brahman* itself. But, according to Sri Chaitanya, though *Brahman* creates the world out of itself, it does not undergo any modification. Even a part of it does not actually the whole. The *parinama-vada* of Sri Chaitanya is called as *sakti-parinama-vada*.

Parinama-vada is the real meaning of the *Sutras* of Sri Vyasa, but it is concealed by the imaginary interpretation of Sankara. The *Sastras* invariably speak of the production of the world from *Brahman*. There is not a single instance in which they have said that the world is a *vivarta* or super-imposition on *Brahman*.

The world is the manifestation of *maya*. But Sri Chaitanya's interpretation of *maya* is essentially different from its Advaitic interpretation by the schools of Sankara. According to Sankara, *maya* is illusion and the world as the product of *maya* is unreal. But he says that *maya* is a potency of *Bhagavan*, and the world as a product of the potency of *Bhagavan*, is real. *Maya* has a two-fold aspect, *Nimitta-maya* or *jiva-maya*, and *upadana-maya* or *guna-maya*. *Nimitta-maya* is the efficient cause of the world, while the *upadana-maya* is its material cause. *Nimitta-maya* has an obvious reference to *jiva*. It has no relation with the eternally free or the *nitya-mukta jivas*. Though Sri Chaitanya believes in *parinama-vada*, according to which the world is a *parinama* or transformation of *Brahman* and not in *vivarta-vada* or illusory appearance of *Brahman*. He emphasizes the reality of the world is relative while the reality of *Brahman* is absolute. *Brahman* does not depend for its existence on anything else, while the world is non-eternal, in the sense that it ceases to exist after dissolution, though eternal in the sense that even after dissolution, it continues to exist in a subtle form in *Brahman*.

Sankara says that the world is a super-imposition *(adhyasa)*. If *Brahman* has something to do with the super-imposition, its *sakti* naturally follows. In *Sruti*, *Brahman* implies greatness as well as expansive activity and *Brahman*, in respect of its expansive activity, is dynamic and *savisesa*. The world is the effect of *ajnana* and is false like *ajnana*. Jiva Gosvami says that if the world is declared as false by Sankara, then what remain to show the existence of *Brahman*? *Brahman* and its *sakti*, which causes the world, are organically related. One cannot be affirmed while denying the other. *Adhyasa* or super-imposition cannot be the subject, because it is included in everything that is negated. *Brahman* cannot be the subject, because it be so, nothing exists besides

Brahman. The knowledge activity of *Brahman* is superimposed or intrinsic.

According to Sri Chaitanya, all the divine forms of Lord *Krsna* are broadly grouped by him under three main heads; *svayam-rupa*, *tadekatma*, and *avesa-rupa*. Jiva Gosvami defines *svayam-rupa* form is that which is self-manifest, that which does not depend upon any other form for manifesting itself. *Tadekatma-rupa* is that which although undifferentiated from the *svayam-rupa* in essence, appears as distinct from it in form, and *avesa-rupa* is that in which Lord *Krsna* manifests Himself by transfusing His power in some favoured *jiva*. Lord *Krsna* has two manifested forms (*svayam-prakasa*), these are *prabhava-prakasa* and *vaibhava-prakasa*.

Prabhava-prakasa is Lord *Krsna*'s simultaneous appearance in many similar forms each dancing separately in the company of one of the innumerable *gopis* in the *rasa* pastime. In the *vaibhava-prakasa* form, Lord *Krsna* manifests Himself as *Balarama*, who is different from Lord *Krsna* only in color, while in every other respect; He is the same as Lord *Krsna*. According to Jiva Gosvami, *goloka* is the *vaibhava-prakasa* of *vrndavana*. He describes *vrndavana* as the inner side of *goloka* and *goloka* as the outer side of *vrndavana*. But they are not the inner or outer side of each other in the physical sense.

Lord *Krsna* is all perfection. His activities are without any motive or conscious effort. *Lila* is either manifest or unmanifest. But this does not mean that there are two different kinds of *lila*. It is the same *lila*, which is called manifest, when it is visible to the phenomenal beings and unmanifest, when it is not visible to them. In the manifest *lila* (*prakata-lila*), there is an appearance of Lord *Krsna's* birth and death, and He grows from infancy to tender youth, while in the unmanifest *lila* (*aprakata-lila*), He is eternally young and there is neither birth nor death. *Aprakata-lila* is a continuous flow. It goes on unimpeded like the continuous flow of time. It is eternal in the sense that it has neither beginning nor end. But though eternal and continuous as a whole, it is not changeless.

Lord *Krsna* is not only the embodiment of bliss but of *rasa*. The word *rasa* is usually translated as 'relish'. It implies both the object that is relished (*asvadya-vastu*) and the person who relishes (*asvadaka*). Lord *Krsna* is both the object that is relished and the person who relishes. In other words, He is both *rasa* and *rasika*. Anything that is relishable or enjoyable is *madhura*. Lord *Krsna* as *rasa* is supremely enjoyable. Therefore, He is *madhura*. *Madhurya* or sweetness is the very essence of His nature. But the *Srutis* describe both *madhurya* and *aisvarya* as equally qualifying the *svarupa-sakti* of *para-brahman Sri Krsna*. *Madhurya* is the intrinsic quality of Lord *Krsna*. *Aisvarya* is His accidental quality. There is no *aisvarya* in the impersonal form of Lord *Krsna*, because it is wholly devoid of *sakti*. But it is not without any *madhurya*. Its *madhurya* manifests itself in the form of *Brahmanda*.

As regards the purpose of His appearance, *Sri Krsna* says in the *Gita* that He appears in every age to protect the good and punish the wicked. But in the *Chaitanya Charitamrta*, it is said that this is not the function of Lord *Krsna*. It is the function of His partial manifest *Visnu*, the sustainer of the universe. The *Srimad Bhagavata* also says that it is not Lord *Krsna*, but His partial manifestations that appear from age to age to relieve the world from sin.

The relation between the *jiva* and *paramatman* is described as that of inconceivable identity-in-difference. It is identity, because *paramatman* is the very source and ground of existence of the *jivas* and they derive their nature as existence, consciousness and bliss from Him. It is difference, because the *jivas* share the nature of *paramatman* in a very small measure. Existence, knowledge, and bliss, in their case, are limited, while in the case of *paramatman*, they are unlimited. This is natural, because *jiva* is atomic consciousness, while *paramatman* is infinite consciousness.

The *jiva* is not simply intelligence or attributeless self-shining consciousness identical with *Brahman*, which is neither knower, nor doer, nor enjoyer as maintained by the Advaitavadins. Though he is a manifestation of the *sakti* of *Brahman*, he has a distinct metaphysical reality of its own, and has knowledge, action and enjoyment as its attributes. According to Jiva Gosvami, the *jiva* is self-luminous (*svayam-prakasa*). Like the light of a lamp, it reveals itself as well as the objects falling within the focus of its consciousness. Its luminosity is derived from *paramatman*, who alone is self-luminous in the real sense. It is called self-luminous only in contrast with the material objects, which neither reveals themselves nor anything else. It is atomic in size. But though atomic, it has the quality of pervading the physical body in which it is temporarily encased.

In the *Chaitanya Charitamrta*, it is said that the manifestations or *avataras* of Lord *Krsna* are the non-differentiated manifestations of Lord *Krsna* (*sva-amsa-rupa*), but the *jivas* are His differentiated partial manifestation (*vibhinna-amsa-rupa*). The *avataras* are the manifestations of His own self, while the *jivas* are the manifestation of His *jiva-sakti* or *tatastha-sakti*. The *tatastha-sakti* is distinct from both *svarupa-sakti* and *maya-sakti*; but is closely connected with them both. The *avataras* share the perfection and power of Lord *Krsna* and are beyond the influence of *maya*. But the *jivas* are subject to the influence of both the *svarupa* and *maya-sakti*. Lord *Krsna*'s birth, and all His other activities are super-natural. His body is not material. It is made of *sat*, *chit*, and *ananda*, and is Eternal. The *Visnu-purana* argues that Lord *Krsna* was not born, but He appeared, because there was no change in Him after His appearance. Before and after His appearance, He was the same—the ground and support of the whole universe. Due to His inconceivable power He appeared in the heart of *Devaki* in a limited form, still He was the same unlimited being as before.

Lord *Krsna* in His 'highest and most perfect form' can be realized only by means of devotion. Those who try to realize Him by *jnana*, perceive Him in His incomplete aspect as *Brahman,* which is but the outward glow or divine luster of His spiritual body. The *Srimad Bhagavata* says that the purpose of Lord's appearance is to impart *bhakti* to the fallen souls (*bhakti-yoga vidhanartha*); not the ordinary type of *bhakti*, which aims at *mukti*, but *raganuga-bhakti*, which consists in intense loving attachment to Lord *Krsna* is called *prema*. *Mukti* can be given by any of the partial manifestations of *Bhagavan* including the *yugavatara*, but *prema* can be given only by Lord *Krsna*. Lord *Krsna* is naturally anxious to impart *raganuga-bhakti*, because He is so merciful and He knows that unless He comes down on earth to impart it, there is no other means by which the *jivas* may attain it and enjoy His unlimited *madhurya*.

Love is essentially dynamic. It is ever growing, ever trying to over reach itself. This is spiritual love or *prema*. Because, Lord *Krsna*'s love is limitless, His hunger for love is also limitless. To satisfy His limitless hunger, His effort is limitless. His descent on earth, time and again, to impart *bhakti* is a result of this effort. He descends to impart *bhakti* in order that He has mere persons to love and to be loved by. Thus the main purpose of His appearance is two-fold. He appears in order that He propagate *raganuga-bhakti* and His devotees enjoy *prema-rasa* as well as His *madhurya*, and in order that He Himself enjoy the *prema-rasa* of His devotees.

Lord *Krsna* as *rasa* is essentially dynamic. Though perfect in all respects, He is always growing and changing in *rasa*.

Mercy is an essential part of His dynamic nature. In every act of mercy He realizes Himself as a better, a higher and a happier self. Every act of mercy for Him is also an act of self-fulfillment and of self-transcendence in bliss.

The inherent weakness of the Advaita philosophy appears in the state of *parama-purusartha* (*kaivalya*). It is described as pure consciousness, which is devoid of the consciousness of self and the not-self, the subject and the object. But there can be no knowledge without a subject.

The attainment of Lord *Krsna* is *moksa*, which means a direct experience of Him. It is either an inward experience in contemplation or an outward experience involving the mind and the senses. The latter experience is higher because it is more vivid and perspicuous.

According to Sri Chaitanya, *moksa* is an end in itself, because it means the attainment of *Bhagavan* in same form or other. If *moksa* is taken in the negative sense of mere cessation of suffering or freedom from bondage, it is not regarded as the ultimate end, but only as a means to it. He defines *mukti* as the attainment of the *jiva's* natural state. In its natural state, *jiva* is a part of *Bhagavan* and its natural function is to serve Him. The attainment of this state implies the attainment of *Bhagavan*, the attainment of bliss, the removal of the influence of *maya* and *karma,* the attainment of a state from where there is no possibility of returning to this world, the cessation of all pain and suffering. But the Advaitins' view that on attaining *mukti*, the *jiva* becomes one with *Brahman* is based on such scriptural texts as *brahma vit brahmaiva bhavati* (*Mundaka*, 111,2,9). The Advaitins maintain that since the *jiva* loses its identity in the state of absorption in *Brahman*, and no subject of experience is left, there is in the *mukti*-bliss, without any feeling or experience of it. The *jiva* becomes bliss, though it cannot experience it. But such a state of *mukti* cannot be prescribed as the highest end, because it is totally uninspiring. Nobody would like to be *mukta*, if *mukti* is devoid of any experience.

Mukti is attained while the *jivas* is in the physical body or after death, when both the physical and subtle bodies destroyed. The later kind of *mukti* is the real end, as it implies complete transcendence of the phenomenal plane and the elimination of all extraneous factors that block the *jivas* inherent capacity to realize the highest kind of bliss. There are five different kinds of *mukti* according to the five different forms in which *Bhagavan* is attained. They are, *sayujya* or absorption in the divine self, *salokya* or attainment of the *loka* or *dhaman* of the deity, *sarupya* or attainment of the form similar to that of the deity worshipped and a place in His *dhaman*, *sarsti* or attainment of the *aisvarya* or power similar to that of the deity, and *samipya* or attainment of proximity to the deity.

The bliss enjoyed in *salokya, sarsti*, and *sarupya-muktis* is superior to the bliss of *sayujya-mukti*, because the *jiva* who attains any of these has his own transcendental body as a *prasada* and is capable of having a more varied experience of the transcendental world by participating in its activities. But the bliss of *samipya-mukti* is even higher, because the *jiva* attains proximity to the deity and enjoys seeing him and his *lila* directly. But this is not possible in *salokya*, *samipya* and *sarsti-muktis*, because in them the *jiva* has only an inward experience of the deity. In *samipya-mukti*, the experience is outward. Outward experience is more vivid and enjoyable. As stated in the *Bhagavata*, Narada Muni went about from place to place singing the praises of the Lord and as he sang *Bhagavan* appeared in his heart, but still he went to *Dvaraka* repeatedly to see Lord *Krsna*, because he found an outward experience of Him much more attractive and pleasing. In this sense, *samipya-mukti* is the highest kind of *mukti*. It implies proximity to *Bhagavan*, he does not fulfill all conditions necessary for His fullest realization, and therefore, the bliss enjoyed by him is also not of the highest order. The reason is that, though outwardly he is near *Bhagavan*, there is something that keeps him at a distance from the care of his heart. That is lack of *priti* or loving devotion, without which real proximity with *Bhagavan*, which means loving intimacy with him is not possible.

Priti is the highest function of the highest *sakti* of *Bhagavan*, namely, the *hladini-sakti*. It implies both the quality of loving and being loved. To realize *Bhagavan* fully, one must realize *priti*, which means that one must realize *Bhagavan* both as object of love and as capable of love Himself. This means that one must realize Him in His *madhura* aspect. But the *jivas* who attain *mukti*, cannot realize in his *madhura* aspect, because their view of *Bhagavan* is dominated by His *aisvarya* and they are not capable of cultivating personal emotional relationship with him.

Epistemology

In Indian philosophical systems, we find and discuss in the history of Indian philosophy that there are six ways of knowing. These are recognized as *perception, inference, comparison, verbal testimony*, *arthapatti* and *anupalabdhi*. Though Sri Chaitanya and his followers gave more importance on *sabda* or *testimony,* but they are not completely denying the other means. Here we discuss the whole concept i.e. Sri Chaitanya's concept of epistemology elaborately.

Jiva Gosvami, in his *Sarva-samvadini*, gives a detailed account of all the traditional sourses of knowledge. Besides *pratyaksa* or *perception*, *anumana* or *inference*, and *sabda* or *verbal testimony*, he mentioned *upama* or *analogy*, *arthapatti* or *implication*, *sambhava* or *equivalence*, *aitihya* or tradition, *arsa* or the words of *Rsis*, *anupalabdhi* or non-recognition, and *chesta* or knowledge derived by physical effort. According to him, *arthapatti* and *sambhava* included under *anumana*, *anupalabdhi, aitihya*, and *chesta* under *pratyaksa* and *arsa* under *sabda*. *Pratyaksa* and *anumana* function as subordinate to *sabda* and not as independent sources of knowledge. So, *sabda* alone is the independent and proper source of knowledge.

Jiva Gosvami mentions two kinds of perception. These are *vaidusa*, which belongs to the learned, or the wise, which are purified by *bhakti*, and *avaidusa*, which belongs to those who are not so purified. *Vaidusa pratyaksa* is the basis of *sabda* itself, being free from all kinds of error, whereas *avaidusa pratyaksa* is liable to error.

One of the western philosophers, Leuba's statement about the relation between theology and psychology shows that Jiva Gosvami's *vaidusa pratyaksa* or the vision of the pure soul is a mystic element in religion. It is not only regarded as something purely subjective, but as indicative of an unhealthy and abnormal attitude of mind. This misconception is due to the vicious use of psychology in religion. Because, psychology can gives us a succession of states in the mind of the mystic; it cannot give us the divine power to initiate, sustain and unify the human being.

Many philosophers limit themselves to perception and inference as the sources of knowledge. According to Sri Chaitanya, perception and inference are defective and unreliable, because they are based on our sense organs. They are influenced by four defects; these are *bhrama* or wrong perception of one thing for another, *pramada* or negligence, *vipralipsa* or proneness to deceive, and *karanapatava* or incapacity of the various sense organs. He says that perception and inference can be treated as valid sources of knowledge when purified by *bhakti*. So, the devoted souls can see the divine personality of Lord *Krsna* to whom the ordinary persons can see.

Sri Chaitanya says that the numinous quality of mystic experience is due to the ingress of *suddha-sattva* in the devotee's consciousness. *Suddha-sattva* is the essence of *sandhini-sakti* or the potency of *God*, which is the ground cause of all kinds of transcendental existence, including the existence of *God* Himself. In the *Chaitanya Charitamrta*, it is said that the validity of mystic experience is illogical, because, it does not submit itself to examination by reasoning.

Purification is a necessary stage in the life of the mystic. It is also the embodiment of an ideal character. Mystic experiences should not be judged by their contents, but by their antecedent spiritual conditions. Sri Chaitanya described about the qualities of a Vaisnava mystic as merciful, harmless, truthful, generous, polite, etc. According to him, a true Vaisnava is like *God* Himself. The immediacy of mystic experience is higher than the immediacy of sense experience. It is an immediacy which is qualified by the mediacy of thought. The realization of truth cannot come through any conceptual system. The mystic completes the work of the philosopher or the theologian. His philosophical or religious doctrine is no longer a doctrine but a life.

Sri Chaitanya's insistence on the character of mystical experience is apparent from his distinction between lower and higher understanding. The lower understanding pertains to ordinary persons and the higher to the sages. He resolves the conflict between subjective experience and objective knowledge through its belief in the ingress of *suddha-sattva*, the principle of transcendental existence. The ingress of *suddha-sattva* in the consciousness of the devotee results in such interpretation of the subject by the transcendental existence that his thought, feeling and will are wholly transformed and sublimated. He comes face to face with truth. The truth is no more an external object of contemplation for him. He not only knows it, but lives it.

The absolute communicates His knowledge in three ways to the finite souls. These three ways are—He sits in their hearts and directs their understanding, He takes the form of the guru or the spiritual preceptor, and helps them through initiation to realize the truth. The guru is the manifest form of the supreme being and an embodiment of His quality of mercy.

The *Srimad Bhagavata* is the foundation of the philosophy of Sri Chaitanya. The contents of the *Srimad Bhagavata* are classified in three heads—*sambandha*, *abhidheya*, and *prayojana*.

Sambandha means relation, treats of the relation between *jiva*, *world* and *isvara*. It primarily means knowledge of the complete personality of *isvara* and *sambandha-prapti*, the realization of our true relationship with Him. *Abhidheya* means the way that leads to the attainment of this relationship, and *prayojana* means the purpose for which the relationship is sought. In this sense, *isvara*, conceived in all His perfection is *sambandha*, *bhakti* is *abhidheya*, and *prema* is *prayojana*.

The *Puranas* and the *Itihasas* are regarded as superior to the *Veda*. Because that are easily understood and are accessible to all. A man who has studied the *Veda* and not the *Itihasa* and Purana, cannot be regarded as truly learned.

Sabda is recognized as the only proper source of knowledge in Sri Chaitanya's philosophy, and the only way to right knowledge is through scriptures. But in Indian tradition, it varies from person to person.

Charvaka system of Indian philosophy accepts *perception* is the only means of valid knowledge. *Inference* and *testimony* are rejected by them, because, *inference* is said to be a mere leap in the dark. *Testimony* too cannot be proved. If *testimony* proves *vyapti, inference* would become dependent on *testimony* and then none would be able to infer anything by himself. Hence neither *inference* nor *testimony* can be regarded as valid source of knowledge.

In Nyaya philosophy, *perception*, *inference*, *comparison*, and *verbal testimony*—all are accepted as valid sources of knowledge. According to them, *sabda* is called as authoritative verbal testimony. It is defined as the statement of a trust worthy person (*aptavakya*) and consists in understanding its meaning.

Mimamsa system accepts five sources; these are *perception*, *inference*, *comparison*, *verbal testimony*, and *implication* are valid sources of knowledge. According to them, *sabda-pramana* has got the greatest importance, and it is the knowledge of the supra-sensible objects which is produced by the comprehension of the meanings of words. Kumarila divides testimony into personal (*pauruseya*) and impersonal (*apauruseya*). The former is the testimony of the trust-worthy persons (*aptavakya*), whereas the latter is the testimony of the *Veda* (*vedavakya*). It is valid in itself. It has intrinsic validity. Vedic injunctions can never be contradicted by any subsequent knowledge. And there can be no internal contradictions in the *Veda* itself. Hence the *Vedic testimony* is valid in itself.

In Vedanta philosophy, Sankara accept *sabda* as the valid source of knowledge. According to him, *Sastra* only generates right knowledge. He gives supreme importance to the revealed truths of the *Vedas* which are regarded as the *Breath of God*.

Ramanuja also accepts *sabda* or verbal testimony as one of the sources of knowledge. He says that the assertive propositions of the *Veda* are as important as the injunctive and the various *karmas* are to be performed only to secure *God's* grace.

Madhva also believed in *Vedic* pramanas, which is classified into two kinds—*apauruseya* and *pauruseya*. *Apauruseya* evidence is derived from the *Vedas*, which include the *Rg Veda*, *Upanisads*, *Mantras*, *Brahmanas*, etc., whereas *pauruseya* evidence is collected from *histories*, *Puranas*, *Pancharatras*, etc. He has full faith in the words of the previous acharyas. Indirectly we can say, he accepts, *sabda* as the source of valid knowledge.

Nimbarka also accept the authority of the *Vedas*. He says that the *Puranas* are the fifth *Veda*. That also clarifies that he accepts *sabda* as the valid source of knowledge.

Vallabha accepts the *scriptures* as the sole authority in spiritual matters. *Scripture* for him is essentially the Veda.

4

Sri Chaitanya on Morality

Morality

Man is a rational animal. Because of his rationality, he is superior to other animals. He has the quality of consciousness. Because of this quality, he is called as an ethical animal. He alone can distinguish between good and bad, vice and virtue, what should and should not, etc. These are some of the predominant attributes (*dharma*) of a human being. Human being is an aggregate of body, mind, and soul. Therefore, *dharma* of a human being is called as *jaiva-dharma* including physical, physiological, psychological and spiritual. Those in whom this quality is absent cannot properly be called a human being. As long as the human being remains pure, he maintains his identity and self-conception in accordance with his unadulterated spiritual function (*sva-dharma*).

According to Sri Chaitanya, in reality, all living beings throughout the universe have only one *dharma*, i.e. *vaisnava-dharma*. Though human beings appeared to be different from their attributes, but by virtue, they are regarded as human being. These attributes are called as *vaisnava-dharma*. Without a *vaisnava-dharma*, a man is not a man, they are simply human beasts. He says that there are two types of human beings or *jivas*, *jnani* (wise), and *ajnani* (ignorant). *Jnanis* can overcome ignorance, whereas *ajnanis* cannot.

According to the nature of the *jiva*, there are two types of human activities, physical activity that relate to practical existence (*vyavaharika*), and spiritual activities that relate to the ultimate goal (*paramarthika*). A person or a Vaisnava's conviction and performance are the two sides of one coin. That means, his thinking or believing reflects in his living. When the *jiva* associated with different types of (*rajasika*, *tamasika* or even *sattvika*) false egoism, his constitutive function becomes perverted. To avoid this, Sri Chaitanya advices for concentrating mind on the lotus feet of Lord *Krsna*, and engage in *Krsna-nama-sankirtana*.

According to him, all the *jivas* are particles of spiritual consciousness. They have a spiritual identity that consists of pure ego, pure consciousness and a spiritual body. When their vision is averted from the Lord and engrossed in illusory material enjoyment, their pure ego and pure consciousness become contaminated with the effects of ignorance. By engaging steadily in the service of *Bhagavan*, the materialistic influence is transformed into the inclination for rendering service to Lord *Krsna*. He realizes his constitutive occupation (*sva-dharma*). At that time, *jiva's* pure consciousness manifests.

It is said in the *Srimad Bhagavatam* that *bhakti* arises from *bhakti* (*bhaktya sanjataya bhaktya*). One must continuously engage in the process of *sadhana-bhakti* through hearing, chanting and so on. By doing this, material enjoyment which is only desirable for a human being will be averted. Though he knows that material enjoyment is the cause of vicious circle of birth and death in this material world, but for a moment he is trapped by *maya*. For getting release of this trap, he makes use of his consciousness and searched an ultimate way, what he found is nothing, but self-surrender to Lord *Krsna*.

Vaisnava-dharma or *jaiva-dharma* is the *nitya-dharma* of a *jiva*. When the *jiva* is liberated from matter, he nurtures

Krsna-prema in his pure spiritual form. Before that stage, when the *jiva* is materially bound although spiritually awakened, he only accepts objects and association that are favorable for his spiritual practice, and he rejects all that is unfavorable.

Manu, a great Vaisnava has said, there are ten characteristics of moral life, for the people who accept moral principles as a sense of duty. These are,

1. *Dhrti* (determination with patience),
2. *Ksama* (forgiveness, which means not retaliating when wronged by others),
3. *Dama* (disciplining of the mind, which means equanimity even in the face of disturbing circumstances),
4. *Asteya* (abstinence from theft),
5. *Saucham* (cleanliness),
6. *Indriya-nigrahah* (restraining the senses from their sense-objects),
7. *Dhi* (intelligence, which means knowledge of the *Sastras*),
8. *Vidya* (wisdom, which means realization of the soul),
9. *Satya* (truthfulness), and
10. *Akrodha* (absence of anger as demonstrated by even temperedness amidst irritating circumstances).

According to Sri Chaitanya, *Bhagavan* is the root of all *dharma*. He is easily conquered by *bhakti*. As soon as *Bhagavan* is established in the heart, *maya*, who binds the *jivas* in illusion, is immediately dissipated. Then the thought of universality comes into his mind. That feeling is expressed through *Krsna-nama-sankirtana*.

When chanting is done audibly with the movement of the lips, it is called as *kirtana*. *Kirtana* is superior to *japa* within the mind, because one derives great benefit by hearing the sound vibration. Sri Chaitanya gives the definition of *sankirtana* as *sarvato bhavena kirtana*, means complete *kirtana*. In other words, *kirtana* that is performed in full knowledge of *sambandha-jnana* and free from all obstructions and offences. This refers to that *kirtana*, the performance of which requires no assistance from any other limbs of *sadhana*. Unalloyed devotion can develop only by continuous engagement in pure *Krsna-nama* in the form of hearing and chanting in the association of unadulterated pure devotees. This *kirtana* also entails freedom from all result-oriented activities.

It is said in the *Chaitanya Charitamrta* that by the performance of *Krsna-nama-sankirtana,* all kinds of impediments to spiritual purification are destroyed and the heart becomes purified. The reactions too many lifetimes of sinful activities are eradicated and along with them, material existence consisting of repeated birth and death, which is a by-product of those sins. All kinds of benedictions arise from *Krsna-nama-sankirtana*.

Apart from all this, there are seven excellent results of *Sri Krsna-nama-sankirtana.* These are,

1. The truth concerning the identity of the living entity is disclosed.
2. By engaging in the service of *Bhagavan*, the greed of the material enjoyment is reduced.
3. Just as the soothing rays of the moon cause the white lotus to bloom, *Sri krsna-nama-sankirtana*, diffusing the moon rays of *bhava-bhakti*, causes the white lotus of good fortune to bloom for the living entities.
4. When unalloyed devotion arises in the heart of the *bhakta* by continuous practice of hearing and chanting, the feeling of *bhakti*, who dispels all

desires other than that for the service of the Lord removes *avidya*.

5. When the gross and subtle bodies of the living entity have been completely destroyed, his infinite nature becomes evident. At that time, on account of the *jiva's* inherent being infinite. It is assumed that his constitutional happiness is also infinite. In other words, Sri Chaitanya says that the holy name is an ever increasing ocean of bliss, which expands the inherent transcendental pleasure of the living entity by virtue of the *hladini* potency.
6. The *jiva*, being eternally situated in one of the transcendental *rasas* of *dasya, sakhya, vatsalya* or *madhurya*, relishes complete nectar at every step by virtue of the ever-increasing freshness of his attachment to Lord *Krsna*.
7. The living entity in the status of *prema* gives unadulterated ecstatic pleasure to Lord *Krsna*. He is devoid of any selfish motives for personal enjoyment. Obtaining one's spiritual form, the *jiva* becomes a maid-servant of *Srimati Radhika*, who is the embodiment of the *hladini* potency and who is always absorbed inn the ecstasy of *mahabhava*. The living entity, thus, tastes unlimited spiritual bliss in connection with the love-sports (*prema-vilasa*) of the divine couple. That means, in the condition of *prema*, Lord *Krsna* is blissful feelings are completely pure.

The Vaisnava ethics springs from the same source as does its theology. It proceeds directly from *bhakti*. The Vaisnavas says, a good man is a true *bhakta* and vice-versa. Mercy towards all creatures (*jiva-daya*) was strongly impressed on Sri Chaitanya's philosophy. It is an aspect of *ahimsa* doctrine which was so congenial to the Vaisnava spirit. The strict vegetarianism that marks the true Vaisnava is a logical expression of this teaching. Humility is the most characteristic feature of the real Vaisnava *bhakta*. It is said in the *Chaitanya Charitamrta* that a *bhakta* although of high position considers he inferior to grass, and acts patiently like the tree. From this example, it is understood that these signs are found in him in whose heart this emotion springs up. He is not affected by worldly afflictions.

According to Sri Chaitanya, character of a Vaisnava is compassionate, free from spite, of the very nature of truth, spotless, charitable, gentle, pure, possessing nothing, doing good to all, peaceful, wholly surrendered to Lord *Krsna,* desire less, harmless, victorious over the six passions, friendly, skillful and silent etc. No doubt the above characteristics of a Vaisnava are not devoid, in any sense, moral conduct or principles.

It is mentioned in the *Siksastaka* that four symptoms are observed in the *bhaktas* who chants the holy name of Lord *Krsna* free from all offences. These are, natural humility born of complete detachment from material sense gratification, pure compassion devoid of envy, purity of heart free from materialistic false ego, and an attitude of respect towards everyone in accordance with their respective position.

When the holy name, which is the personification of transcendental rasa, makes its appearance in the heart of the *bhakta*, it overwhelms his heart and begins to think that I am by nature infinitely conscious and a servant of Lord *Krsna.* I have no use of mundane material objects. Due to my apathy towards Lord *Krsna,* I now find myself in a miserable plight. My ego in respect to the present subtle and gross material bodies is fundamentally wrong. The ego of grass is real, but my material ego is unreal. Therefore, it is proper for me to become even lower than a blade of grass. I have now understood that my indifference can be dissipated only by executing the *sadhana* of devotion unto the supreme Lord. Then he becomes so merciful than a tree. Like a tree, he does to all—both friend and enemy. He is free from ego, which arising from mystic powers, material opulence, wealth, beauty, social status, strength, etc. He offers respect to everyone as befits their respective position. He never thinks this material world for his own enjoyment. He saw everything in this world as related to Lord *Krsna*. All moving entities as servants of Lord *Krsna* and non-moving entities as enjoyable by Lord *Krsna*.

For a *jiva* or a Vaisnava, heavenly objects are desire less and worthless, it is confirmed in the *Srimad Bhagavatam*. He should endeavor to attain devotion which is purely unmotivated. He not only rejects material enjoyment in the form of religiosity, accumulation of wealth, sense-enjoyment, and he rejects desirer for liberation also. He does not have desire to serve Lord *Krsna* for obtaining these goals. He desires to serve Him only for His own pleasure.

5

The Main Tenets of Ramanuja Philosophy

In Ramanuja Philosophy, the supreme *Brahman* has been accepted as one without a second. It is full of transcendental qualities. The non-dual *Brahman* alone is the cause and effect of all other objects. He is the cause of creation, maintenance, and destruction of the material world. He is the director of the cosmic manifestation, free from all abomination, the abode of all auspicious, extremely pleasant, etc.

Ramanuja says that Lord *Narayana*, the husband of *Laksmi*, alone is the supreme personality of Godhead. *Brahman* is *God*. He is not a form less identity to which Sankara denies. According to him, the absolute *Brahman* is an organic unity, an identity which is qualified by diversity. His concept of *God* is identified with the absolute. He is *Brahman*. He must be a *savisesa* or a qualified unity. He stands for the whole universe, and matters and souls from His body, He being their soul. During the state of dissolution, *God* remains as the cause with subtle matter, and during the state of creation, the subtle matter becomes manifest. *God* is considered as the immanent inner controller of this world process.

The supreme personality of Godhead has full of transcendental knowledge and possessor of unlimited potencies. He is the only shelter of all kinds of living entities. Besides this, Ramanuja recognizes three things as ultimate and real (*tattva-traya*). These are *matter* (*achit*), *soul*s (*chit*), and *God (isvara*). Though all are equally real, but the first two are absolutely dependent on the third one, i.e. *God*.

The supreme soul and the individual spirit souls are not completely identical, but the conception of oneness between them exists. The material body and the spirit soul are both directly and indirectly connected with the super soul. But, according to Ramanuja, it does not indicate that the body and soul are identical with the super soul in all respects. According to him, one should revive his relationship with the supreme soul by spiritual cultivation only. One should worship and meditate to the supreme personality of Godhead with love and devotion while remaining fixed in the principle of *varnasrama-dharma*. It must be our ultimate goal of life, nothing else.

Knowledge and detachment from matter are automatically attained by engagement in pure devotional service, which means the supreme Lord is served by pure living entities through the rendering of devotional services. One who has actually perfect in the acquisition of knowledge engages in the devotional service of the Lord.

Ramanuja and his followers emphasizes on *prapatti* (self-surrender) as the easiest and surest means of liberation. For them, *prapatti* is also called as *saranagati*. It itself is real *bhakti*. They distinguish between *prapatti* and *bhakti* in the sense that the highest *bhakti* is not with emotional love of *God*, but with the immediate intuitive knowledge of *God*. Liberation, according to him, is not the merging of the individual soul into the absolute, but only the direct intuitive realization by the individual soul of its own essential nature as a mode of *God*. For him, there is no *jivan-mukti* for as long as the soul remains associated with the body, the soul cannot acquire its innate purity. And there is no liberation without *God's* grace for unless the divine grace dawns. The liberated soul does not become identical with *Brahman*, but only similar to *Brahman* (*Brahma-prakara*). It realizes itself as the body of *Brahman*.

In the liberated state, all spirit souls have equal qualities and nature. Because, the living entities are the minute parts and parcels of the supreme Lord. The supreme Lord or controller is the complete whole and the living entities are His fragmented parts and parcels.

Comparative Study with Sri Chaitanya Philosophy

The supreme *Hari* is one without a second. Lord *Hari* or *Sri Krsna* is eternal, spiritually true. The highest, best and the most spiritual ideas of the divinity is Lord *Krsna*. He has infinite powers. His powers are identified with His person. His power has an attribute to exhibit perfectly spiritual existences. Though His power is not distinguishable from the person of that being, but the powers are separately exhibited in their separate actions. This is called as inconceivable simultaneous existence of distinction and non-distinction.

According to Sri Chaitanya, Lord *Krsna* is only the supreme personality of Godhead. He has names, forms, and qualities like other individual souls. The absolute *Brahman* is neither one, nor two, nor in between one and two, nor beyond one-and-two. The status of absolute *Brahman*, Lord *Krsna* is unthinkable, i.e. *achintya-tattva*. But Jiva Gosvami has given a different meaning of the word *achintya,* is incapable of being considered under either of the categories of absolute difference and absolute non-difference. Like Ramanuja, Sri Chaitanya also accepted the concept of *God* is identified with the absolute. He has forms, qualities, names, etc. like other human beings. But He is different from them because of His transcendental qualities, like *sat-chid-ananda*.

The supreme personality of Godhead is the shelter of all the *jivas*. He has three real energies or *saktis*, these are *svarupa sakti*, *tatastha* or *jiva sakti*, and *bahiranga sakti*. He described Lord *Krsna* as the only ultimate reality and other living and non-living beings are the modifications of His energies.

The relation between *Brahman* and the *Universe* is neither identity, nor difference, nor of identity-in-difference. It is rather a form of qualified non-dualism, in which, the components stand in *achintya* or supra-luminal relation. He admits the reality of the world. Though the material body and the individual souls are the manifestations of *God* or the energies of *God*, but they are not different from *God*, they are not also identical with *God*.

According to Sri Chaitanya, the only aim of our life is to serve *God* or to worship *God* through dancing and chanting the names of Lord *Krsna* with unadulterated pure devotees, to which he named as *nama-sankirtana*. That is the only way to relate with Lord *Krsna*. Once you surrender yourself to *God*, then nobody else comes in between you and *God*. Then the question of attachment with worldly matters, detachment from your duties, knowledge, etc. is meaningless. There is no obstruction like caste, class, or anything else for worshiping or serving *God*. So, to become a devotee, knowledge does not play any role.

Bhakti is the only means for attaining the final object of spiritual existence. *Karma* cannot directly and immediately produce spiritual result. When it does, it does by means of *bhakti*. Hence, *bhakti* is independent, where as *karma* and *jnana* are dependent principles. *Jnana* or knowledge cannot bring the ultimate object. When it does, it does with the assistance of *bhakti*. *Bhakti*, therefore, is the only means to obtain the ultimatum. It is defined as the cultivation of a friendly sentiment for Lord *Krsna*. *Bhakti* is itself both a feeling and an action.

When the *jiva* coming under the influence of *maya-sakti*, forgets his spiritual nature and gets identified with materiality, but he never loses his essential spiritual attributes. When the obstructing veils of *maya-sakti* are removed through *bhakti*, then he became liberated. They may lose their sense of individual existence in the bliss of divine communion, but this does not mean that their distinctive entity is lost.

Out of the three energies of Lord *Krsna*, the individual soul or the *jiva* has taken only the sat quality or energy at the time of creation from *Brahman*, but at the time of dissolution or liberation, internally he is identical with *Brahman*. That means the quality or the energies of Lord *Krsna* and the individual souls are same.

The Philosophical Problems of Sri Chaitanya and Ramanuja

Like Chaitanya, Ramanuja also refuted Sankara's *absolutism* (*Brahmavada*). They tell us that as per Sankara's absolutism, *God* is not a *God* at all. Their *God* possesses super-natural divine qualities, viz. *sat-chid-ananda*. The supreme personality of Godhead, Lord *Krsna* is not unlimited, what Ramanuja described, but have only *tatastha* or *jiva-sakti* and *bahiranga-sakti*.

Ramanuja's importance on the service of the Vaisnavas than the supreme personality of Godhead is criticized by Sri Chaitanya. He says that the service of the Lord *Krsna* is our ultimate goal of life. So, you should dedicate yourself to Lord *Krsna*. It is also mentioned in a similar way in the *Bhagavad Gita*. You worship Lord *Krsna* through dancing and chanting His divine names.

Unlike Sri Chaitanya, like Vallabha, Ramanuja could not appreciate the wonderful excellence of the worship of *Radha-Krsna*. According to him, Lord *Narayana*, the husband of *Laksmi*, is the supreme personality of Godhead.

Ramanuja's concept of *prapatti* is not their in Sri Chaitanya's philosophy, though its representation is in a different way. Ramanuja's concept of *prapatti* is self-surrender; whereas Sri Chaitanya's concept of *nama-sankirtana* is to pray *God* with chanting and dancing with the help of musical instruments. It is also another form of self-surrender yourself to *God*. In Sandilya's outlook, we also find the highest type of *bhakti*, which are *bhajana* and other phases are component parts of it.

Ramanuja gives more importance on *dasya-rasa*, where as Sri Chaitanya gives importance on *madhura-rasa*. Because for him, both *Radha* and *Krsna* are one and undivided divine soul. So, their divine love should be worshipped, and their love is *madhura-prema*. According to Sri Chaitanya, though their bodies are not one, but their soul is one *(avicchedya-anga)*.

Regarding the acquisition of perfect knowledge, Parasara Muni says that the path of perfection is nothing more than activities performed for the pleasure of the supreme Lord. This path is to be traversed step by step; it is obtained only by engagement in devotional service, and this path can be ascertained by a thorough study of ancient literatures, such as the *Vedas*, and *Vedanta-sutra*. But Sri Chaitanya does not agree on this point by saying that to know about the (perfection of) knowledge of the *Vedas* or the *Vedanta-sutra*, it is very much necessary to obtain *God*'s grace.

The Main Tenets of Madhva Philosophy

In Madhva Sampradaya, Lord *Visnu* is the supreme personality of Godhead. He is unlimited, faultless and full of transcendental qualities. He is omnipotent, fully independent, the controller of all moving and non-moving living entities. He is *sacchidananda vigraha*. There is no difference between His body and His soul. His names, forms, qualities and pastimes are all transcendental. He is the controller of all controllers. Those who differentiate between the forms, qualities, and pastimes of the incarnations of the Lord, will certainly be forced to enter darkest regions of hell. According to them, Lord *Hari* is also the supreme absolute truth. He is fully spiritual and eternal. He is completely independent. He possesses a form with hands, legs, etc. and all his bodily limbs are manifestations of His blissful nature. His appearance, growth, disappearance are not caused by the influence of material time, place or circumstance. He creates, maintains and annihilates the material world by His independent will. He manifests unlimited eternal forms in the spiritual world.

The living entities are separate from Lord *Visnu*. They are the servants of Lord *Hari*. They are also present in *vaikuntha* as reflections of the transcendental forms of the supreme Lord. There is a similarity between the form and quality of the supreme soul and the individual soul. The difference between them is that in the individual soul, the knowledge and bliss are partial, where as the knowledge and bliss of the supreme soul is full. He is the origin of all existences.

The material world is real. He, like Ramanuja, believes in *God*, *soul* and *matter* as the three real entities. The souls and matter are absolutely dependent on *God*. *God* is the Lord of *karma*. He pleased only by *bhakti*. He manifests Himself in various incarnations. *Laksmi* is His concert. She is all-pervading and eternal like Him, but Her qualities are little lesser than of Her Lord.

Lord *Visnu* is the master of *maya*. The living entities, who mare eligible for entering the next creation as a result of their previous *karma* are placed within the creation. But by worshipping the infallible supreme personality of Godhead with unalloyed devotion, people can attain the state of liberation in this world. They never fall down again. According to their advancement in spiritual knowledge, they gradually attain proximity to the supreme Lord. Out of four kinds of liberation (*salokya, samipya, sarupya* and *sayujya*), *sayujya-mukti* is most important. Because *Brahma* alone can attain *sayujya-mukti.* Literally, *sayujya* means to enter the body of Lord *Visnu*, just as a ghost may enter a person's body.

Madhva emphasizes the difference of the liberated *soul* from *God*. He says, the *soul* becomes similar to *God* in some respects when it is liberated, but he does not enjoy the full bliss of *God.* According to him, *bhakti* is the only means of liberation. It is defined as the eternal love for *God* with a full sense of His greatness. But he accepts that the realization of the supreme Lord is also possible by cultivating the spiritual knowledge that comes down in disciplic succession. According to him, liberation is not a condition imposed upon the individual living entities. It is also mentioned in the *Vedas* that the knowledge that awards liberation is nothing but transcendental knowledge of the supreme Lord.

Worship of the demigods is prohibited in Madhva sampradaya. As long as one is in good health and his senses are active, he should engage in the worship of Lord *Hari*, and thus, make his life perfect, Madhva says. He, like Ramanuja accepts the three sources of knowledge, these are, *perception*, *inference* and *testimony*.

Comparative Study with Sri Chaitanya Philosophy

In Sri Chaitanya's sampradaya, the ultimate reality is Lord *Krsna*. He is infinite and all-pervading. He is perfect and eternal. Though He has infinite manifestations in various names and forms, but He is one. Lord *Krsna,* the supreme being possesses a name and form like a human being. But He is different from them in the sense that He has transcendental qualities which is absent in a human being.

According to Sri Chaitanya, the relation between the living entities and the supreme soul is neither identical, nor difference, nor both identical-cum-difference. It is unthinkable, inconceivable, unimaginable, unpredictable, etc. That's why; Sri Chaitanya's philosophy is called as *'achintya bhedabheda-tattva'*.

Though there is some similarity between the forms and qualities of the supreme soul and the individual soul, but the difference between them is that the supreme soul has transcendental qualities, like *Sat-Chit-Ananda*, where as the individual soul have only empirical qualities.

According to him, the material world is real. Because, this world is the real manifestation of the supreme Lord. He also accepts that everything happens because of *karma* and it is under the control of supreme Lord.

According to Sri Chaitanya, *karma* means Vedic ritualistic action. It is either of an obligatory nature or of an optional nature for attainment of heavenly enjoyments. Vedic rituals are detained from devotional rituals, which is the *bhakti* discipline. But discharge of one's duties in selflessness and detachment has a place in the devotee's life, as it leads to the purification of his mind through the elimination of the demoniac tendencies born of self-centeredness. Thereby, it increases the competence of the aspirant to follow the specific *bhakti* disciplines. But then such *karma* is a part and parcel of *bhakti* discipline, and it should be distinguished from the pursuit of *Vedic karma*.

The individual devotees being of the nature of *God* (when the sense of their inner selves, like existent, sentient and blissful nature awakened) have every right to relish its company which is exemplified by the intense love play with his Vrndavana associates.

According to Sri Chaitanya, *bhakti* is the only means to please *God*. Other means like *karma*, *yoga*, *jnana,* etc. are not the direct or primary means to obtain the grace of *God*. The path of *yoga* or concentration may be considered as an independent path for *jiva* to lead to the *Paramatman*, the intermediate aspect of the divine as the seat of all power and glory, just like the path of *jnana*, this also is a diversion from the goal of the highest felicity that is *bhakti*. He never denied worshiping demigods, though he regularly visited the temple of *Visvesvara*, who was predominating deity of Varanasi.

Sri Chaitanya says that *sabda* or *sruti* as the valid authority, but he also accepts the supremacy of *sabda-pramana*. Sri Chaitanya accepts five kinds of liberation or *mukti*. These are—*salokya*, *sarupya*, *sarsti*, *samipya* and *sayujya*.

The Philosophical Problems of Sri Chaitanya and Madhva

Like Ramanuja, Madhva also believed that the supreme being and His energies are *Visnu* and *Laksmi* respectively. They represent the *aisvarya* or the aspect of power pomp, greatness and command respect and devotion of the *jivas*. That means, *God* and His devotees have some difference. But in Sri Chaitanya's philosophy, the human relation between *God* and His devotees is more important. In the Vrndavana sports of the *God*, the *jivas* find in him as a friend, a son, or a lover. Instead of *aisvarya*, the *madhurya* or the aspect of human tenderness is given more prominence.

Madhva discards the theories of other Vedantins. He is a pure dualist. Madhva Vaisnavism is a Brahmanical religion, where as Gaudiya Vaisnavism in their theory as well as in their practice, consider a Vaisnava not by birth, but on his depth of devotion. They say, those who identify a Vaisnava with his caste (birth) will be drowned into the lowest hell after his death.

Sri Chaitanya accepts Isvara Puri as his guru, although he belonged to Madhva sampradaya. It has been also seen that Gaudiya Vaisnavas are known as *Brahma-Madhva-Gaudiya-Sampradaya*, though Gaudiya Vaisnavism is principally quite different from Madhva sampradaya as they are having their own doctrine of a*chintya bhedabheda*.

Both Sri Chaitanya and Madhva agreed on the point that guru's grace is most essential for one's spiritual progress. Unlike Sri Chaitanya, Madhva gives more importance to the service of the Vaisnavas.

Instead of Four kinds of liberation of Madhva, Sri Chaitanya and his followers accept Five, these are, *salokya, sarupya, samipya, sarsti*, and *sayujya-mukti.*

The Main Tenets of Nimbarka Philosophy

According to Nimbarka, the supreme absolute truth is Lord *Krsna*. He possesses an eternal, transcendental body. He is spotless. He is supremely independent, omnipotent, the controller of all controllers. He is the source of all beauty and sweetness. He appears as the supreme personality of Godhead before the eyes of devoted transcendentalists.

The individual spirit souls and the supreme soul are simultaneously one and different from each other. The individual soul is essentially of the nature of knowledge. It is also the substratum of knowledge. It is eternal and yet it suffers births and deaths on account of its embodiment which is due to *karma* and *avidya.*

Matter and souls are the parts and powers of *God*. They are both directly and indirectly related to the supreme Lord. When the living entities are conditioned by *maya*, they are covered by gross and subtle bodies, but when they are liberated, they become freed from these coverings.

It is the duty of all living beings to worship Lord *Krsna*. Those who worship the demigods rather than Lord *Visnu* are considered travelers on the path to hell. Indirectly, Nimbarka wants to show that worship of the demigods is prohibited.

The illusory energy *maya* is eternal. Liberation is due to knowledge which is brought about by *God*'s grace which itself is due to devotion. To know things in truth is real knowledge, Nimbarka says. He accepts the *Vedas* as the crest jewel of all evidences. He also accepts the supplementary Vedic literatures as evidence.

Comparative Study with Sri Chaitanya Philosophy

The supreme absolute truth is no other than Lord *Krsna*, whose self is a form resembling that of a human being, but in reality, He is infinite and all-pervading. He is perfect, eternal. He has infinite manifestations, but He is one and the same self though appears as many.

The individual soul and the supreme soul are neither identical nor different nor both. Their relation is *achintya*, unthinkable. They both are one in one sense (*svarupa-laksana*), and not one in another sense (*bahiranga-laksana*). The individual souls in essence are the servitors of Lord *Krsna*. But Lord *Krsna* has three-fold real *saktis*, these are *svarupa*, *tatastha* or *jiva* and *bahiranga-sakti*. So, matter and souls are the energies of Lord *Krsna*.

When the *jiva* stands in between the material power (*maya*) and spiritual power (*chit*), he gets into the state of bondage. That means, the *maya-sakti* dominates over him and makes him purely body minded. But when through the practice of devotion and the grace of the Lord, he is enfolded by the *svarupa-sakti*, the same as *chit-sakti* of the Lord, and then he attains to his higher spiritual evolution.

Service of the Lord *Krsna* is man's ultimate goal. Sri Chaitanya never mentioned any where that worshipping other beings than Lord *Krsna* is the subject to the path to hell. According to him, anything which exists in this world is real. But he rejects the *maya-vada* theory of Sankara and it's off spring, the doctrine of super-imposition. He says that *maya*, a mysterious power of manifestation which cannot be described categorically either as sat or as *asat* or as *abhava-rupa*. So, *maya* itself become *achintya*.

An individual soul got liberation due to the grace of *God*, not through knowledge. That's why, Sri Chaitanya says that somewhere that to become a devotee, it is not necessary to know or to read *Veda*. According to him, the knowledge which got from the scriptures is right or perfect knowledge. He also accepts the *Veda*s, the *Vedanta-sutra* and *Prasthana-traya* are the authentic sources.

The Philosophical Problems of Sri Chaitanya and Nimbarka

No doubt, Nimbarka sampradaya introduced the worship of *Radha-Krsna*, but for the Gaudiya Vaisnava sampradaya, *Radha* characteristic super-excellently shines forth. Besides this, it is shown only in Gaudiya sampradaya that the love of *Sri Radha* for *Sri Krsna* has brought unique theory.

Nimbarka, like Ramanuja admits *God*, *souls* and *matter* are the three realities, where as Sri Chaitanya admits only Lord *Krsna* is real and others are His energies. Nimbarka's concept of the relation between *jiva* and *God* is that, *jivas* are both distinct and non-distinct from *Brahman*. This concept is very close to Sri Chaitanya philosophy. Nimbarka accepts six-fold *prapatti* and nine-fold *bhakti* to give up all *karmas* for the service of *God*. He also accepts five-fold relational service to *God* as Gaudiya Vaisnavas emphatically give stress upon *santa*, *dasya*, *vatsalya*, *sakhya*, and *madhurya* relationships with *God*.

Gaudiya Vaisnavas accept *love-in-relation* and *love-in-separation*. But this mode of *love-in-separation* is not found in the Nimbarka sampradaya. Further, the five-fold relational service of Nimbarka sampradaya is found only in *Dasa-sloki*, which seems to be of latter origin and not given by Nimbarka himself. Most probably this system of philosophy is borrowed by them from Gaudiya Vaisnavas.

Regarding Nimbarka's concept of *liberation*, Sri Chaitanya differs from him, in the sense that an individual soul got liberation only through *God*'s grace, not by any other means.

Although Nimbarka philosophy, in some respect, indebted to Ramanuja, but he differs from them also. For example, Ramanuja believes in *identity-in-and-through-difference* or *identity-qualified by-difference*. But Nimbarka believes in *identity and difference*. Where as Madhva's philosophy is *pure dualism* and Nimbarka's philosophy is both *dualism-cum-absolutism,* and Sri Chaitanya's philosophy is *unthinkable dualism-cum-absolutism*, where as Nimbarka's philosophy is simple *dualism-cum-absolutism*.

The Main Tenets of Vallabha Philosophy

The transcendental *Brahman* or *Purusottama* is identical with Lord *Krsna*. Lord *Krsna* is both the supreme person and the absolute being. He is the source of the *jivas* and the world of matter. Matter does not mean anything different from *Brahman*. *Brahman* is not only the *nimitta-karana* (efficient cause) of this universe; He is also its *samavayi-karana* (inherent cause). Vallabha does not admit the *maya-vada* theory of Sankara, where as he admits the existence of ignorance, but its action is held to be quite different from Sankara.

The *jivas* are the parts of *Brahman*. *God*'s creation of the *jivas* and the *jagat* is absolutely real. They are the very *Brahman* Himself without His *chit* and *ananda* nature. The world manifested by *Brahman* is actually there and not imagined to be their by any one because of *avidya*. Vallabha accepts the doctrine of super-imposition. He says that the *jiva* owing to *avidya* or ignorance generated by desires and attachments makes a wrong and perverse evaluation of the world, taking an ego-centric or self-centered view of what is really the Lord's playful manifestation. The world is in no sense generated by the *jivas*' super-imposition. It is the real manifestation of *sacchidananda parabrahman*.

Vallabha distinguishes between *jagat* or *prapancha* and *samsara*. According to him, *jagat* is the real manifestation of *God*, while *samsara* or the cycle of births and deaths is imagined by the soul on account of ignorance. *Maya* can be only *Brahman*'s real power, producing real effects and not false appearances.

Vallabha says that *bhakti* as a firm and self-surpassing affection (*sneha*) for *God* with a full sense of His Greatness is the only means of salvation. It is the loving service of *God*. It means attachment to *God* which pre-supposes detachment from all other things. It is neither worship nor knowledge. Affection or *prema* is its dominant phase. *Vatsalya* or parental form of devotion is the most favored form of love practiced in worship.

The practice of *seva*, both in its physical and mental aspects, brings devotion to maturity when it takes the form of *asakti* or intense attachment to *God*. The devotee is a part and parcel of divine life. He is in union with the heart and the spirit of *God*. Service with body and wealth has taken the form of serving *God* in images. Devotion is only a means for *God*'s grace *for maryada-jiva*, but for the *pusti-jiva*, it is both the means and the end. The duty of *pada-seva* is an integral part of the Vaisnava discipline. When one gets fully established in this attitude, one transcends *samsara*, even in its noblest form, namely, as self-centered devotion consisting in the aspiration for *moksa* for oneself and use of devotion as means to it.

The *scripture* is the sole authority in spiritual matters. *Reason* has no place in it.

Comparative Study with Sri Chaitanya Philosophy

Like Vallabha, Sri Chaitanya also says that the transcendental *Brahman* is identical with Lord *Krsna*. He is both the supreme person and the absolute being. He is the source of the *jivas* and the world of matter. *Brahman* is the material as well as the efficient cause of the *universe*. But He transforms Himself into the *universe* remaining unaffected by the transformation.

The *jivas* are both identical and different from *Brahman*. He is the energy or potency of the Lord. Just as *sakti* and *saktimat* are one and not different. When the *jiva* coming under the influence of *maya-sakti*, forgets his spiritual nature and gets identified with materiality, but he never loses his essential spiritual attributes.

Though the supreme personality of Godhead, Lord *Krsna* is only real and other entities are only the modifications (*parinama*) of His energies. So, the world is the modification of Lord *Krsna*'s energies (*bahiranga-sakti*). The world, the *jivas* and other both living and non-living entities are real in their own stand point and they perform their duties according to their own status or position.

According to Sri Chaitanya, when the interest of the *jiva* or soul is shifted from his individual self to the spiritual whole and finds fulfillment in entire submission and loving service of Him, is called as *bhakti*. In this sense, it is an end in itself. It is distinguished from *mukti* or liberation. *Mukti* is union with the supreme. Sri Chaitanya gives more importance on *madhurya-prema* (*bhakti*) than others. According to him, *bhakti* or devotion is both the means as well as end in itself. Not simply self-surrender, *nama-sankirtana* with a group of unadulterated pure devotees is the main way to serve Lord *Krsna*. Though Sri Chaitanya described the nine-fold means of practicing *bhakti* (*navadha-bhakti*), but according to him, *nama-sankirtana* is superior to others.

The Philosophical Problems of Sri Chaitanya and Vallabha

Like Sri Chaitanya, Vallabha also accepted that *Brahman* is identified with Lord *Krsna*. But his philosophy is different from Sri Chaitanya in the point that soul and matter are the real manifestations of Lord *Krsna*. But the *achintya bhedabheda* theory of Sri Chaitanya accepts the wider view regarding the relation of *sakti* and *saktimat,* which is different both from *Brahma-vivartavada* (transfiguration of *Brahma*) of Sankara and *Brahma-parinamavada* (transformation of *Brahma*) of Ramanuja. According to the former, the world as it appears, has no separate existence apart from *Brahman*, while according to the latter, the world as it is real, is due to the fact that *Brahman* changes itself into the world. Contesting both the views, the *achintya* doctrine upholds a new concept of *sakti-parinamavada* (transformation of *sakti*) which is not found in any other philosophical system. Sri Chaitanya's response for this is that, the world is *achit* and *jivas* is the transformation of *Brahman*, who is the shelter of *chit-sakti*, *jiva-sakti* and *maya-sakti*. So, these *saktis* are regarded as *achintya-jnana-yogachara*, i.e. falling within the range of inexplicable knowledge.

Vallabha accepted souls and matter are His parts. At the same time, he also described *Brahman* as one as well as many and it is by His will that He manifests Himself as matter and as souls revealing His tripartite nature of existence, knowledge and bliss. But Sri Chaitanya does not agree with Vallabha on this point. He says that though Vallabha accepts souls and matter are the real manifestations of *Brahman*, but this view is neither *parinama* nor *vivarta*. It is something in between the two, which is called as *avikrta-parinama-vada*.

Though Vallabha described Lord *Krsna* as *para-brahman*, *purusottama*, *sacchidananda brahman,* but like Sri Chaitanya, he does not accept the female figure *Radha* with Lord *Krsna*. He admitted Lord *Krsna* as a shephered boy of Vraja with Gopis, but a female figure worshipped with *Krsna* is only called *svamini*. In this respect, Vallabha's philosophy and Sri Chaitanya's philosophy are different.

Vallabha's philosophy not only different from Sri Chaitanya, he also differs from other Vedantic philosophies. His argument is that, if *Brahman* is *nirvisesa* (quality less), then what is the status of *maya*? Is it external to *Brahman* or internal with *Brahman*? If it is an internal part of *Brahman*, then *Brahman,* of Sankara, is not *nirvisesa.* If it is external, then it will be just like the *Prakrti* of Sankhya, an independent dynamic substrate of evolution. Then it clearly shows that the reality is not one, but two. In this respect, he criticizes other philosophies who believes in-between. That's why, Vallabha's philosophy is pure non-dualism (*suddhadvaita*).

Vallabha rejects the relation of substance with attributes as *samavaya*, and explains it as *tadatmya* or identity. He uses the word s*amavaya* in the sense of material cause and that means the inherent cause which suggests that the material cause is identical with its effect, and does not involve in it. Vallabha's conception of *jagat* and *samsara* is different from Sri Chaitanya's conception. According to him, *avidya* or ignorance generates *samsara* and the world is in no sense generated by the *jivas*' super-imposition. It is the real manifestation of *sat-chid-ananda para-brahman.*

The doctrine of grace or *pusti* has given Vallabha's system a distinctiveness of its own among the various Vaisnava schools of thought. All the Vaisnava schools accepted the nine forms of devotional disciplines mentioned in the *Bhagavata-purana*, and for them the first six items, i.e. *sravana*, *kirtana*, *smarana*, *pada-sevana*, *archana,* and *vandana* are practiced as preliminary disciplines or *apara-bhakti*, by which one gets gradually spontaneous love of *God* without any external stimulation, and become capable of practicing devotional attitudes and self-surrender, where as the final stages are called as *para-bhakti*. But Vallabha recognized that this graduated discipline is for *maryada* or for the low-bound *jivas*. Those who belong to the *pusti*-group, they start with the last. Grace of *God* can achieve what the effort of man cannot. But in Sri Chaitanya's philosophy, the most important form of love is *madhura-bhava*, which is openly and predominately preached by him, but it is not accepted by Vallabha in the same manner. He says that the love of the Gopikas has nothing sexual as understood in this world. It is *dasya-bhava*, the nature of servitude to *God*, which is the most sublime intimate form. It is *alaukika* of which sex love as seen in the world is a perversion. So, one must have the grace of *God* even to understand and appreciate it in the proper light.

Conclusion

All the traditional Vaisnava schools, irrespective of their different philosophical doctrines, made a common opposition against Sankaras absolutism (*maya-vadism*). All of them accepted Lord *Visnu* (in His different forms) as the supreme *God* with His divine names, forms, and attributes, and *bhakti* is the means to attain Him and the *jiva* souls are the eternal servitors of Him.

Due to Sri Chaitanya's pilgrimage cum preaching tour over almost all the vaisnava stronghold centers in the country and his personal contact with many of the sampradaya acharyas, his divine magnanimity and clear conception of *God*, particularly his ecstatic devotional chanting of *Krsna-nama* and philosophical deliberations worked a great deal to make the followers of the sampradayas to be attracted and subscribe to certain extent his devotional cult of *Radha-Krsna* and chanting of divine *Krsna-nama*.

The theology of the Gaudiya Vaisnavas has certain exceptional features which are not found in any other Vaisnava schools of thought. The theme of *Sri Radha* as *hladini-sakti* and Her transcendental love with *Sri Krsna* is the special theme and unique in *Gaudiya Vaisnavism*.

Sri Sandilya's philosophical outlook is similar with a*chintya bhedabheda tattva* of Sri Chaitanya. To him, the highest type of *bhakti* is *bhajana* and other phases are component parts of it. Both Narada and Sandilya emphatically proclaimed that *bhakti* is unparalled and unprecedented. *Karma* and *jnana* have got their relative values when they are in conformity with the *bhakti*. In this sense, they both are also close to the philosophy of Sri Chaitanya.

The path of devotion is for the change of the innermost attitude. It is from materialism to *God*-centered attitude. It is from selfishness to altruistic love. It is a path from exclusiveness to pluralism. It also goes beyond pluralism as it ends into a pathless land. It accommodates all diversities as its foundation is love, divine love and not hatred. It is going beyond all finitudes and freedom from limitations. It is the realization that the divinity is beyond any diversity. As states in *Yajur-veda* that it is the experience of the universe becoming one single house. It is the experience of prayers becoming one, it is the unity with one mind; there is universality in the prayers of *bhaktas*. They do not pray for their own religion, language, caste, and creed. They pray for the entire humanity. The commonality is strong.

But Sri Chaitanya's *bhakti* movement brought about a glorious literary renaissance is a very well-known fact. The society itself grew mobile. Literacy was spread among the low-caste people. *Brahmanical smrti* and the tradition of *Panchopasana* had not produced comparable results. This shows that the *bhakti*-movement of Sri Chaitanya was, at least in its initial stages, neither morbid nor intellectually supine. Had it been so, it would not have produced a single positive result. The principle of individuality implied by *bhakti* was quite dynamic. It lent vitality to the moribund society in Bengal. Emotion was necessary for a people downtrodden for many centuries. And creative without it the wonderful literary and architectural renaissance would not have occurred at all. Especially for the Chaitanyas, writes Max Weber, "the basis of *bhakti* was recognized to be the coarse sexual orgiasticism of the masses, accompanying cultivation of the earth, and thereby was itself of a sexual-orgiastic character". Weber does not know that Sri Chaitanya and the gosvamins of Vrndavana never preached mere eroticism. In fact, they preached the virtues of the ascetic way of life. *Madhura-rati*, no doubt, is an erotic concept. But the *madhura-rati* contemplation was not compulsory for all *bhaktas*. They could freely worship Lord *Krsna* as a master, as a friend, and even as their son. Sexual orgiasticism was not the ideal or the aim of the *bhakti* movement of Sri Chaitanya. Even Weber admits that the true *bhakta* adherent of impure thought and drives particularly anger, envy, and desire. This inner purity gave certitude solutes. This occurred particularly in the intellectual strat.

The *bhakti* movement of Sri Chaitanya emphasized the theory of surrender of the self to *God* or to the guru. The Gaudiya Vaisnava devotee was, according to S.N. Dasgupta, advised to absolve *God* of the responsibility for his own misery, because *God* cannot have experience of it; and so, in spite of *God*'s omnipotence, yet, since He has no experience of the suffering of men, he cannot be accused of cruelty in not releasing everyone from his suffering. When *God* tries to satisfy the desires of his devotee, he is not actuated by an experience of suffering, but by an experience of the devotion existing in the devotee. Thus, no trust is placed in the bhaktas individual capacity to affect either material or spiritual improvement. Only his *bhakti* is active. All other things are passive. This doctrine could not bring about any social or economic revolution. *Bhakti* is regarded by an interpreter of Hinduism as an accurate reflection of the chronic helplessness of the Indian masses.

It is believed that *bhakti,* greatly influenced the rise of Maratha power, Ancient authority and tradition had been petrified in western Indian regions in what Mahadev Govinda Ranade described as the monopoly of the Brahmin caste. It was against the exclusive spirit of this caste domination that the saints and prophets struggled most. They asserted the dignity of the human soul. The leaders of the *bhakti* movement were primarily interested in the dissemination of the values of Hinduism (which had till then remained confined to the Brahmana castes) among the lower and middle castes through expressing them in a language, and in an idiom comprehensible to the common people. They sought to create social cohesion by directing the allegiance of the various castes to a common corpus of religious values. The aim of *bhakti* was to create social-cohesion, not social revolution.

Bibliography

Abhyankar, Vasudeva Sastri (eds.) (1951), *Sarva-Darsana-Sangraha of Madhavacharya,* Bhandarkar Oriental Research Institute, Poona.

Acharya, Dr. Mrs. Kala (eds.) (2003), *The Bhakti: Pathway to God*, Somaiya Publications Pvt. Ltd., Mumbai.

Agarwal, M.M. (eds.) (2000), *The Philosophy of Nimbarka*, Bhargava Book House, Agra.

Agrawal, Madan Mohan (1983), *The Philosophy of Nimbarka*, Chaukhamba Surbharati Prakashan, Varanasi.

Appaswamy, A.J. (1970), *The Theology of Hindu Bhakti*, Christian Literature Society, Madras.

Aurobindo, Shri (1950), *Essays on the Gita,* The Sri Aurobindo Library, New York.

Bahirat, B.P. (1956), *The Philosophy of Jnanadeva*, Motilal Banarsidass, Delhi.

Bapat, Shailaja (2004), *A Study of the Vedanta in the Light of Brahmasutras*, New Bharatiya Book Corpn., Delhi.

Barz, Richard (1976), *The Bhakti Sect of Vallabhacarya,* Thomas Press Ltd., Haryana.

Basham, A.L. (1967), *The Wonder that was India: A Survey of the History and Culture of the Indian Sub-Continent Before the Coming of the Muslims,* Sidgwick and Jackson, London.

Bhaktivedanta Swami, A.C. (1973), *Sri Caitanya Caritamrta*, Vol. 2, The Bhaktivedanta Book Trust, Los Angeles.

Bhaktivedanta Swami, A.C. (1974), *Sri Caitanya Caritamrta*, Vol.1, The Bhaktivedanta Book Trust, Los Angeles.

Bhaktivedanta Swami, A.C. (1991), *Narada-Bhakti-Sutra*, The Bhaktivedanta Book Trust, Bombay.

Bhaktivedanta Swami, A.C. (1999), *Vedic Philosophy for Students*, Sri Sri Sitaram Seva Trust, New Delhi.

Bhaktivedanta, Swami, A.C. (1968), *Teachings of Lord Caitanya: A Treatise on Factual Spiritual Life*, International Society for Krishna Consciousness, New York.

Bhandarkar, R.G. (1982), *Vaisnavism, Saivism, and Minor Religious Systems*, Vol. IV, Bhandarkar Oriental Research Institute, Poona.

Bhandarkar, R.G. (1965), *Vaisnavism, Saivism and Other Minor Religious Systems*, Indological Book House, Varanasi.

Bharadwaj, Krishna Datta (1958), *The Philosophy of Ramanuja*, Sri Shankar Lall Charitable Trust Society, New Delhi.

Bharati, S. (1968), *Alvar Saints and Acharyas,* Shuddhananda Library, Madras.

Bhatta, S.R. (1975), *Studies in Ramanuja Vedanta,* Heritage Publishers, New Delhi.

Bhattacharya, N.N. (1989), *Medieval Bhakti Movements in India: Sri Caitanya Quincentenary Commemoratum Volume,* (eds.), Munshiram Manoharlal Publishers Pvt. Ltd., New Delhi.

Bhattacharya, S.A. (1961), *A Study of the Cult of Devotion*, Adyar Library Bulletin, Madras.

Bloomfield, M. (1908), *The Religion of the Veda*, G.P. Putnam and Sons, New York.

Bouquet, A.C. (1962), *Hinduism*, Hutchinson & Co. Ltd., London.

Bowes, Pratima (1976), *The Hindu Religious Tradition: A Philosophical Approach*, Allied Publishers Pvt. Ltd., Mumbai.

Brockington, J.L. (1997), *The Sacred Thread: A Short History of Hinduism*, Oxford University Press, New Delhi.

Carpenter, J.E. (1921), *Theism in Medieval India*, Allen and Unwin Ltd., London.

Carpenter, Joseph Estlin (1921), *Theism in Medieval India*, The Hibbert Lectures (2nd Series 1921), Williams and Norgate, London. (Reprinted New Delhi 1977).

Carpenter, Joseph Estlin (1997), *Origin and Development of Religion in India,* Sanjay Prakashan, Delhi.

Chaitanya, Svarupa (1982), *Tattva Bodha of Sankaracharya*, Central Chinmaya Mission Trust, Bombay.

Chakravarti, S.C. (1969), *Philosophical Foundation of Bengal Vaisnavism*, Academy Publishers, Calcutta.

Chakravarty, Dr. Ramakanta (1985), *Vaisnavism in Bengal (1486-1900)*, Sanskrit Pustak Bhandar, Calcutta.

Chandra, Satish (1996), *Historiography, Religion and State in Medieval India*, Har-Ananda Publications, New Delhi.

Chandra, Satish (1997), *Medieval India: From Sultanat to the Mughals*, Har-Anand Publications Pvt. Ltd., New Delhi.

Chari, S.M. Srinivasa (1994), *Vaisnavism: Its Philosophy, Theology and Religious Discipline*, Motilal Banarsidass Publishers Pvt. Ltd., New Delhi.

Chari, S.M. Srinivasa (1976), *Advaita and Visistadvaita*, Motilal Banarsidass Publishers Pvt. Ltd., New Delhi.

Chatterjee, A.N. (1983), *Srikrisna Caitanya: A Historical Study on Gaudiya Vaisnavism*, Associated Publishers, New Delhi.

Chatterjee, Rama (1985), *Religion in Bengal*, Punthi Pustak, Calcutta.

Chaudhuri, R. (1953), *The Nimbarka School of Vedanta*, Cultural Heritage of India, Calcutta.

Chennakesavan, S. (1976), *Concepts of Indian Philosophy*, Orient Longman, New Delhi.

Chowdhary, Roma, *Doctrine of Nimbarka and His Followers*, 3 Vols., Pub. RASB. Co. Pvt. Ltd., New Delhi.

Chaudhury, Roma (1962), *Ten Schools of the Vedanta*, I, II, III, Rabindra Bharati University, Calcutta.

Comans Michael (1998) (Tr.), *Advaitamoda by Vasudevashastri Abhyankar, A Study of Advaita and Visistadvaita*, Sri Satguru Publications, Delhi.

Comstock, W. Richard (1972) (ed.), *Religion and Man: An Introduction*, Harper and Row Publishers, Inc., New York.

Das, Sain (1953), *Message of the Upanisads*, Atmaram and Sons, Delhi.

Dasgupta, S.N. (1922, 1932), *A History of Indian Philosophy* (Vols. 1, 2 & 4), Cambridge University Press, London.

De, S.K. (1942), *Early History of the Vaishnava Faith and Movement in Bengal,* Ancient Indian Erotics and Erotic Literature, Calcutta.

De, Sushil Kumar (1961), *Early History of the Vaisnava Faith and Movement in Bengal,* Firma K.L. Mukhopadhyay, Calcutta.

Deussen, Paul (1908), *The Philosophy of the Upanisads,* (Trans.), A.S. Geden, T. & T. Clook, Endinburgh.

Dhavamony, Mariasusai (1971), *Love of God According to Saiva Siddhanta: A Study in the Mysticism and Theology of Saivism*, Ely House, Oxford University Press, London.

Dr. Kumudini (2001), *Doctrines of Samkarabhasya and Bhaskarabhasya on Brahmasutras*, Vidyanidhi Prakashan, Delhi.

Dutta, D.M. (1970), *Chief Currents of Contemporary Philosophy*, Calcatta University, Calcutta.

Dutta, D.M. (1974), *Six Ways of Knowing*, Calcatta University, Calcutta.

Edgerton, F. (1965), *The Bhagavadgita*, Harper Torch Books, New York.

Farquhar, J.N. (1920), *An Outlines of the Religious Literature of India*, Humphrey Milford, London.

Farquhar, J.N. (1967), *Modern Religious Movements in India*, Munshiram Manoharlal Publishers Pvt. Ltd., New Delhi.

Fuller, C.J. (1992), *The Camphor Flame: Popular Hinduism and Society in India*, Princeton University Press, Oxford.

Gambhirananda, Swami (1998), *Bhagavad Gita of Madhusudana Saraswat I (With the Annotation Gudhartha Dipika)*, (trns.), Advaita Ashrama, Calcutta.

George, A.M. (1978), *Bhakti Andolan aur Sahitya*, Pragati Prakashan, Agra.

Ghate, V.S. (1926), *The Vedanta*, B.O.R.I., Poona.

Ghurye, G.S. (1953), (eds.) *Indian Sadhus*, Popular Prakashan, Bombay.

Gonda, Jan (1977), *Medieval Religious Literature in Sanskrit*, (Vol. 2, Fisc. 1), Otto Harrassowitz, Wiesbaden.

Gosvami, Bhagabat Kumar (1922), *The Bhakti Cult in Ancient India*, Advaita Ashram, Calcutta.

Gosvami, Jiva (1937), *Bhakti Sandarbha,* (eds. Prana Gopal Gosvami), Navadveep.

Gosvami, Rupa (1888), *Bhakti Rasamrita Sindhu,* (eds. Ramnarayan Vaidya Ratna), Murshidabad.

Gosvami, Srila Bhaktisiddhanta Sarasvati (2007), *The Life and Teachings of The Four Acaryas*, Jai Nitai Press, Vrindavan.

Goswami, Asha (2001), *The Krishna Legend: A New Perspective,* Y.R. Publications, Delhi.

Goswami, B.K. (1965), *The Bhakti Cult in Ancient India*, (2nd eds.), Varanasi.

Govindacharya, Sri (1898), *Bhagavat Gita with Ramanuja's Commentary* (Trans.), Vaijayanti Press, Madras.

Goyal, S.R. (1986), *A Religious History of Ancient India (Upto C. 1200)*, Vol. 2, Kusumanjali Prakashan, Meerut.

Grimes, John (1990), *The Seven Great Untenables*, Motilal Banarsidass, Delhi.

Gupta, Din Dayal (1970), *Ashtachhap aur Vallabha Sampradaya*, 2 Vols., Hindi Sahitya Sammelan, Allahabad.

Gupta, Dr. Shanti Swarup (Edited) (1982), *Religion: A Solution of Modern Problems*, Dharma, Oxford University Press, Delhi.

Habib, Irfan (1965), *The Historical Background of the Popular Monotheistic Movements of the 15th-17th Century,* (Paper presentation) Delhi University, Delhi.

Hardy, Friedhelm (1983), *Viraha-Bhakti: The Early History of Krisna Devotion in South India*, Oxford University Press, Delhi.

Hastings, James (1909, 1964), *Encyclopaedia of Religion and Ethics,* Vols. 2 & 4, (eds.) T. & T. Clark, New York.

Hasurkar, Dr. S.S. (1958), *Vacaspati Misra on Advaita Vedanta,* Mithila Institute of Post-Graduate Studies and Research in Sanskrit Learning, Darbhanga.

Hinnells, John R. and Sharpe, Eric J. (eds.) (1972), *Hinduism?*, Oriel Press Ltd., England.

Hiriyana, M. (1952), *Popular Essays in Indian Philosophy*, Kavyalaya Publishers, Mysore.

Hiriyana, M. (1967), *Outlines of Indian Philosophy,* George and Unwin Ltd., London.

Hopkins, E.W. (1911), *The Epic use of Bhagavat and Bhakti*, Journal of Royal Asiatic Society, New Delhi.

Hopkins, E.W. (1956), *The Natural History of Religion*, Adams and Charles Black, London.

Hopkins, E.W. (1977), *The Religions of India*, Ginn and Co., Boston House, New Delhi.

Husain, Yusuf (1933), *The Influence of Islam on the Cult of Bhakti in Medieval India,* Indian Culture, Vol. VII, Delhi.

Husain, Yusuf (1957), *Glimpses of Medieval Indian Culture*, Asia Publishing House, Bombay.

Iyer, Dr. S. Venkitasubramonia (1977), *Religion Art and Culture*, College Book House, New Delhi.

Jackson, William J. (2004), *Soul Images in Hindu Traditions: Patterns East and West,* B.R.

Jagadeesan, Dr. N. (1977), *History of Sri Vaishanavism in the Tamil Country*, Koodal Publishers, Madurai.

Jaiswal, Suvira (1980), *The Origin and Development of Vaisnavism (Vaisnavism from 200 B.C. to A.D. 500)*, Munshiram Manoharlal, Delhi.

Jayamal, K. (2003), *A Glossary of Technical terms in the Commentary of Sankara, Ramanuja and Madhva on the Brahma-Sutras*, Vol. 1 & 2, ICPR, New Delhi.

Kapoor, Subodha (2002) (Ed.) Encyclopedia of Vedanta Philosophy, Vols. 1-5, Cosmos Publications Pvt. Ltd., New Delhi.

Kapoor, O.B.L. (1977), *The Philosophy and Religion of Sri Caitanya*, Munshiram Manoharlal Publishers Pvt. Ltd., New Delhi.

Keith, A.B. (1925), *The Religion and the philosophy of the Veda and the Upanisads,* Harvard University Press, Cambridge.

Kennedy, Melville T. (1925), *The Chaitanya Movement: A Study of Vaishnavism in Bengal*, Munshiram Manoharlal Publishers Pvt. Ltd., New Delhi.

Kinsley, David R. (1979), (eds.) *The Divine Player: A Study of Krsna Lila*, Motilal Banarsidass Publishers Pvt. Ltd., Delhi.

Krishna Swami, M.N. (1998), *Golden Men and Their Golden Word's,* Rashtriya Sanskrit Sansthan, New Delhi.

Krishna, Daya, Lath, Mukund & Krishna, Francine E. (eds.) (2000), *Bhakti: A Contemporary Discussion,* ICPR, New Delhi.

Krishnarao, C.R. (1929), *Sri Madhva, His Life and Doctrine*, Prabhakara Press, Udipi.

Kumar, Shashi Prabha (1999), *Facts of Indian Philosophical Thought*, Vidyanidhi Prakashan, Delhi.

Kumarappa, Bharatan (1934), *The Hindu Conception of the Deity as Culminating in Ramanuja,* Luzac, London.

Kumarswamiji (1957), *The Cultural Heritage of India*, Advaita Ashram, Calcutta.

Lata, Prem (1980), *Mystic Saints of India: Ramanuja*, Sumit Publications, New Delhi.

Lahiri, Dr. Aloka (1993), *Chaitanya Movement in Eastern India*, Punthi Pustak, Kolkata.

Latif, Syed Abdul (1958), *An Outline of the Cultural History of India*, (eds.), The Institute of Indo-Middle East Cultural Studies, Hyderabad.

Lester, R.G. (1966), *Ramanuja and Sri-Vaisnavism: The Concept of Prapatti or Sarangat in History of Religions*, Chicago.

Luniya, B.N. (1978), *Life and Culture in Medieval India*, Kamal Prakashan, Indore.

Macdonald, K.S. (1982), *The Vedic Religion*, Sanskrit Pustak Bhandar, Calcutta.

Macnicol, Nicol (1915), *Indian Theism from the Vedic to the Muhammadan Period*, Oxford University Press, Oxford.

Madhavananda, Swami (2000), *Viveka Cudamani of Sri Sankaracarya*, (trns.), Advaita Ashrama, Calcutta.

Madhavananda, Swami (1993), *Uddhava Gita*, Advaita Ashrama, Calcutta.

Madhusudana Sarasvati (1984), *Bhakti-rasayana*, Acyuta-grantha-mala, Kasi.

Mahadevan, T.M.P. (1956), *Outlines of Hinduism*, Chetana Ltd, Bombay.

Majumdar, A.K. (1965), *Bhakti Renaissance*, Bharatiya Vidya Bhavan, Bombay.

Majumdar, A.K. (1969), *Caitanya: His Life and Doctrine: A Study in Vaisnavism*, Bharatiya Vidya Bhavan, Bombay.

Majumdar, R.C. (1960), *The History and Culture of the Indian People*, Vol. VI (eds.), Bharatiya Vidya Bhavan, Bombay.

Malik, Muhammad (1971), *Vaishnava Bhakti Andolan ka Adhyayan*, Rajpal & Sons, Delhi.

Mallik, G.N. (1927), *The Philosophy of Vaisnava Religion*, Motilal Banarasi Das, Lahore.

Manikar, T.G. (1980), *The Making of the Vedanta*, Ajanta Publications, Delhi.

Marfatia, M.I. (1967), *The Philosophy of Vallabhacharya*, Munshiram Manoharlal, Delhi.

Max Muller, Fredrick (1894), *Three Lectures on the Vedanta Philosophy,* Longmans, London.

Mishra, A.P. (1967), *The Development and Place of Bhakti in Sankara's Vedanta*, Sanskrit Deptt. University of Allahabad, Allahabad.

Mishra, Umesha (1940), *Nimbarka School of Vedanta,* University of Allahabad, Allahabad.

Misra, Sudama (1973), *Janapada State in Ancient India*, Bharatiya Vidya Prakasana, Varanasi.

Mohan Singh (1934), *Kabir and Bhakti Movement*, Atma Ram, Lahore.

Morgan, K.W. (1953), *The Religion of the Hindus,* Ronald Press, New York.

Mukherjee, Prabhat (1981), *The History of Medieval Vaisnavism in Orissa*, Asian Educational Services, New Delhi.

Mukherji, Dr. S.C. (1966), *A Study of Vaisnavism in Ancient and Medieval Bengal*, Punthi Pustak, Calcutta.

Muni Narayana Prasad, Swami (1991), *Basic Lessons on India's Wisdom*, Narayana Gurukula, Kerala.

Murthy, H.V. Sreenivasa (1973), *Vaisnavism of Samkaradeva and Ramanuja: A Comparative Study*, Motilal Banarsidass, Delhi.

Murty, K. Satchidananda (1986), Sad-Darsana Samuccaya (A Compendium of Six Philosophies), Eastern Book Linkers, Delhi.

Murty, K. Satchidananda (1985), *Philosophy in India: Traditions, Teaching & Research*, (ICPR), Motilal Banarsidass, Delhi.

Nahar, Ratibhanu Singh, *Bhakti Andolan ka Adhyayan,* Kitab Mahal, Allahabad.

Narada and Sandilya, *Bhakti Sutra,* Advaita Ashram, Calcutta.

Narain, K. (1962), *An Outline of Madhva Philosophy*, Udayana Publications, Allahabad. (Reprinted New Delhi, 1986)

Narain, K. (1964), *A Critique of Madhva Refutation of Sankara School of Vedanta*, Udayana Pub., Allahabad.

Narang, Dr. Sudesh (1984), *The Vaisnava Philosophy*, Nag Publishers, Delhi.

Nath, Narendra (1949), *Sri Krsna and Sri Caitanya*, Luzac & Co., London.

Nayak, G.C. (1978), *Essay in Analytical Philosophy*, Santosh Publication, Cuttack.

Neog, Maheswar (1965), *Sankaradeva and His Times: Early History of the Vaisnava Faith and Movement in Assam*, Gauhati University, Department of Publication, Gauhati.

Nikhilananda, Swami (1959), *Vedanta Sara or The Essence of Vedanta of Sadananda Yogindra,* Advaita Ashrama, Calcutta.

Nikhilananda, Swami (1968), *Mandukya Upanisad with Gaudapada Karika and Sankara's Commentary,* Sri Ramakrisna Math, Mysore.

Nityagopal (1953), *The Philosophy of Union by Devotion*, Mahabirban Math, West Bengal.

Nizami, K.A. (1966), *Studies in Medieval Indian History and Culture*, Kitab Mahal, Allahabad.

Noel Seth, S.J. (1984), *The Divinity of Krishna*, Munshiram Manoharlal Publishers Pvt. Ltd., New Delhi.

Pai, Dr. D.A. (1928), (Edited by Dr. Pushpendra Kumar) *Religious Sects in Ancient India: Ancient &Medieval,* Eastern Book Linkers, New Delhi.

Pal, Bipinchandra (1933), *Bengal Vaishanavism*, Modern Book Agency, Kolkata.

Pande, Sasmita (1989), *Medieval Bhakti Movement: Its History and Philosophy*, Kusumanjali Publications, New Delhi.

Pandey, Ramnarayan (1966), *Bhakti Kavya mein Rahasyavada,* National Publishing House, Delhi.

Pandurangi, K.T. (1995), *Dvaita Vedanta Darsana of Sri Madhavacharya*, Rshtriya Sanskrit Sansthan, New Delhi.

Parekh, M.C. (1979), *Shri Vallabhacharya: Life, Teachings, and Movement*, Shri Bhagavata Dharma Mission, Rajkot.

Parrinder, Geoffrey (1970), *Avatar and Incarnation,* Faber and Faber, London.

Pattnaik, Tandra (eds.) (2006), *Bhakti*, Department of Special Assistance in Philosophy, U.U., Bhubaneswar.

Paul, Manmath Nath (1911), *Sandilya-Bhakti-Sutra* (Text with trns.) Indian Press, Allahabad.

Philips, Maurice (1887), *The Evolution of Hinduism*, Asian Publication Services, New Delhi.

Pike, E. Royston (1951), *Encyclopaedia of Religion and Religions,* George Allen & Unwin Ltd., London.

Plott, John C. (1974), *A Philosophy of Devotion: A Comparative Study of Bhakti and Prapatti in Visistadvaita*, Motilal Banarsidass, Delhi.

Poddar, Hanumanprasad, (1947) (eds.), *The Philosophy of Love*, Ghanshyamdas Jalan: Gorakhpur.

Poitwin, Guy & Raikar, Hema (1995), *Stone Mill and Bhakti,* D.K. Printworld Pvt. Ltd., New Delhi.

Potter, Karl H. (1981), *Encyclopedia of Indian Philosophies*, Vol. 3, Motilal Banarsidass Publishers Pvt. Ltd., Delhi.

Poona, A.R. (2002) (eds.), *Studies in Vedanta Philosophy*, Bharatiya Kala Prakashan, Delhi.

Prabhupada, A.C. Bhaktivedanta Swami (1980), *Teachings of Lord Caitanya: The Golden Avatar,* The Bhaktivedanta Book Trust International Inc., Mumbai.

Prabhupada, A.C. Bhaktivedanta Swami (1997), *The Quest for Enlightenment,* The Bhaktivedanta Book Trust International Inc., Mumbai.

Radhakrishnan (1967), *Religion in a Changing World,* A George and Unwin Ltd., New York.

Radhakrishnan (1983), *Indian Philosophy*, Vol. 2, A George and Unwin Publication, New Delhi.

Radhakrishnan, S. (1953), *The Principal Upanisads* (Trans.) Notes etc., Harper, New York.

Radhakrishnan, S. (1960), *The Bhagavat Gita* (Trans.) Notes etc., Allen and Unwin, London.

Radhakrishnan, S. (1977), *Visistadvaita*, University of Madras, Madras.

Radhakrishnan, S. (1923, 1927), *Indian Philosophy* (2 Vols.), Allen and Unwin, London.

Raghavacharya, S.S. (1969), *Sri Ramanuja on the Gita*, Sri Ramakrishna Ashram, Mangalore.

Raghavacharya, V. (1956), *Historical Evolution of Sri Vaisnavism in South India* , Cultural Heritage of India, Calcutta.

Raghavan, A.S. (2003), *Visistadvaita*, Executive Officer, TTD, Tirupati.

Raghavan, V.L.S.N. (1979), *History of Visistadvaita Literature,* Ajanta Publication, Delhi.

Raghavendracar, H.N. (1941), *Dvaita Philosophy and its Place in Vedanta*, Mysore University, Mysore.

Ramaiah, G. Sundara (1974), *Brahman: A Comparative Study of the Philosophies of Sankara and Ramanuja,* Andhra University, Waltair.

Ramanuja, Acarya (1916), *Sri-bhasya*, Reprinted from the Pandita, Banares.

Ranganathananda, Swami (1991), *Eternal Values in a Changing Society*, Bharatiya Vidya Bhavan, Bombay.

Ranganathnanda, Swami (1987), *Eternal Values for a Changing Society*, Vol. I, Bharatiya Vidya Bhavan, Mumbai.

Rao, Nagaraja (1960), *Introduction to Vedanta*, Bharatiya Vidya Bhavan, Mumbai.

Rashid, A. (1969), *Society and Culture in Medieval India,* (1st eds.), Firma K.L. Mukhopadhyaya, Calcutta.

Raychaudhuri, H.C. (1920), *Materials for the Study of the Early History of the Vaishnava Sect*, Cultural Heritage of India, Calcutta.

Reddington (1984), *Vallabhacharya and the Love Games of Krsna*, Advaita Ashram, Calcutta.

Renou, Louis (1961), (eds.) *Hinduism*, Prentice-Hall Int., London.

Rupa Gosvami (1988), *Hari-bhakti-rasamrta-sindhu*, Acyuta-grantha-mala, Kasi.

Sadananda (1949), *Vedanta-sara,* 3rd eds., Almora.

Sahukar, Mani (1966), (eds.) *Sweetness and Light: An Exposition of Sati Godavari Mataji's...*, Samaj College Publications, Aligarh.

Sandilya (1912), *Bhakti-sutra,* Panini Office, Allahabad.

Saraswati, Swami Satyananda (1977), *Sannyasa Tantra*, Bihar School of Yoga, Bihar.

Saraswati, Swami Vidyananda (2001), *The Brahmasutra: The Philosophy of God-Realisation*, Vijaykumar Govindram Hasanand, Delhi.

Sarkar, Jadunath (trns.) (1988), *Caitanya's Life and Teachings (From his Contemporary Bengali Biography the Chaitanya-charit-amrita),*Orient Longman, Calcutta.

Sastri, K.A. (1960-62), *Nilakanta, Vaishnavism and the Early Alvars*, Advaita Ashram, Calcutta.

Sastri, Prof. Asoke Chatterjee (1992), *Caitanyabhagavata: A Study*, Nag Publication, Delhi.

Satprakasananda, Swami (1965), *Methods of Knowledge According to Advaita Vedanta*, Advaita Ashram, Calcutta.

Sen, Dinesh Chandra (1922), *Chaitanya and His Age*, Advaita Ashram, Calcutta.

Sen, K.M. (1961), *Hinduism*, Penguin Books Ltd., England.

Sengupta, A.A. (1976), *A Critical Study of the Philosophy of Ramanuja*, Chowkhamba, Varanasi.

Shah, J.G. (1969), *Shri Vallabhacharya: His Philosophy and Religion*, Pustimargiya Pustakalaya, Nadiad.

Shanbhad, D.N. (1982), *Some Problems in Dvaita Philosphy in Their Dialectical Setting*, Sri Rama Prakashan, Dharwad.

Shanbhag, D.N. (1990), Sri Madhvacarya and His Cardinal Doctrines, Bharat Book Depot and Prakashan, Dharwad.

Sharma, A. (1978), *Visistadvaita Vedanta: A Study*, Heritage, New Delhi.

Sharma, B.N.K. (1934), *Svatantradvaita or Madhva's Theistic Realism*, G.S. Press, Madras.

Sharma. B.N.K. (1979), *Sri Madhva's Teachings in his Own Words*, Bharatiya Vidya Bhawan, Bombay.

Sharma, B.N.K. (1962), *Philosophy of Sri Madhavacarya*, Motilal Banarsi Dass Publishers Pvt. Ltd., Delhi.

Sharma, B.N.K. (1981), *History of Dvaita School of Vedanta and its Literature,* Motilal Banarsidass, Delhi.

Sharma, C.D. (1994), *A Critical Survey of Indian Philosophy,* Motilal Banarsidass, Delhi.

Sharma, D.S. (1991), (eds.) *What is Hinduism?*, V.K. Publishing House, Delhi.

Sharma, Krishna (1987), *Bhakti and the Bhakti Movement: A New Perspective, A Study in the History of Ideas*, Munshiram Manoharlal Publishers Pvt. Ltd., Delhi.

Sharma, Munshi Ram (1953), *Bhakti ka Vikas*, Chowkhamba, Banaras.

Sharma, R.S. (1969), *Social Change in Early Medieval India*, Heritage, Delhi.

Sharma, Suman (1974), *Madhya Kalin Bhakti Andolan ka Samajik Vivechan,* University Press, Varanasi.

Shaw, Purnananda (1990), *Morality and Religion in Advaita and Visistadvaita*, Deputy Publications, Delhi.

Siddhantashastree, Rabindra Kumar (1985), *Vaisnavism Through the Ages*, Munshiram Manoharlal Publishers Pvt. Ltd., New Delhi.

Sihna, Jadunath (1956), *Bhagavata Religion: The Cult of Bhakti* in Cultural Heritage of India, Calcutta.

Sihna, Jadunath (1973), *The Philosophy of Nimbarka*, Sihna Publishing House, Calcutta.

Sihna, Nandlal (1911), *Narada-Bhakti-Sutra* (Text with English trns.), Indian Press, Allahabad.

Singer, Milton (1966), *Krishna: Myths, Rites, and Attitudes,* East-West Center Press, Honolulu.

Sinha, Debabrata (1983), *The Metaphysics of Experience In Advaita Vedanta: A Phenomenal Approach*, Motilal Banarsidass, Delhi.

Sinha, Dr. Priti (1986), *The Philosophy of Adavaita (A Transition from Sankara to Sri Aurobindo)*, Sivaraja Publications, Varanasi.

Sinha, Jadunath (1973), *The Philosophy of Nimbarka*, Sinha Publishing House (P) Ltd., Kolkata.

Sircar, D.C. (1971), *Studies in the Religious Life of Ancient and Medieval India*, Motilal Banarsidass, Delhi.

Sircar, M.N. (1927), *Comparative Studies in Vedantism,* Oxford University Press, Oxford.

Sivananda, Sri Swami (1961), *About Hinduism*, The Sivananda Literature Research Institute, Uttar Pradesh.

Sivananda, Sri Swami (1984) (eds.), *Bhakti and Sankirtan*, The Divine Life Society, Uttar Pradesh.

Sivananda, Sri Swami (1986) (eds.), *Voice of the Himalayas*, The Divine Life Society, Uttar Pradesh.

Snatak, Vijayendra (1957), *Radha Vallabha Sampradaya: Sidhhanta aur Sahitya,* Anusandhan Parishad, National Publishing House, Delhi.

Solomon, T.J. (1970), *Early Vaisnava Bhakti and its Autochthonous Heritage*, History of India, Delhi.

Srikripaluji Maharaja, Jagataguru (2002), *Prema Rasa Sidhanta*, Radha Govind Samiti, New Delhi.

Srinivasachari, P.N. (1946), *The Philosophy of Visistadvaita,* Adyar Library, Madras.

Srinivasachari, P.N. (1952), *A Synthetic View of Vedanta,* (2nd eds.) Adyar Library, Madras.

Srinivasachari, P.N. (1972), *The Philosophy of Bhedabheda*, Adyar Library, Madras.

Srinivasachari, S.M. (1976), *Advaita and Visistaadvaita: A Study based on Vedantadesika's Satadusanai*, Motilal Banarsi Dass, Delhi.

Srinivasachari, S.M. (1988), *Fundamentals of Visistadvaita Vedanta,* Motilal Banarsidass, Delhi.

Swarup, Ram (2000), *Meditations: Yogas, Gods, Religion*, Voice of India, New Delhi.

Tapasyananda, Swami (1990), *The Glory of Bhakti: Bhakti Schools of Vedanta*, Sri Ramakrishna Math, Madras.

Tyagisananda, Swami (1978), *Narada Bhakti Sutras*, Sri Ramakrishna Math, Madras.

Tapasyananda, Swami (1992), *Sri Nimbarka: His Life, Religion and Philosophy*, Sri Ramakrishna Math, Madras.

Tapasyananda, Swami (1992), Sri *Vallabhacarya: His Life, Religion and Philosophy,* Sri Ramakrishna Math, Madras.

Tapasyananda, Swami (1995), Sri *Caitanya Mahaprabhu: His Life, Religion and Philosophy*, Sri Ramakrishna Math, Madras.

Tapasyananda, Swami (1996), Sri *Madhvacarya: His Life, Religion and Philosophy*, Sri Ramakrishna Math, Madras.

Tapasyananda, Swami (1996), Sri *Ramanuja: His Life, Religion and Philosophy*, Sri Ramakrishna Math, Madras.

Tarachand (1963), *Influence of Islam on Indian Culture*, Indian Press, Allahabad.

Tattwananda, Swami, *Vaisnava Sects, Saiva Sects, Mother Worship*, Nirmalendu Bikash Sen Gupta, Calcutta.

Thakura, Srila Bhaktivinoda (2004), *Jaiva Dharma*, Gaudiya Vedanta Publications, Bangalore.

Thirugnanasambandhan, P. (1969-70), *The Concept of Bhakti,* (eds.), University of Madras, Trivandrum.

Tyagisananda, Swami (1983), *Narada Bhakti-sutras*, Sri Ramakrisna Math, Madras.

Upadhyaya, Dr. Shukaratna (2000), *Bhakti-Rasa-Sidhanta*, B.S. Sharma & Brothers, Agra.

Vaidya, C.M. (1980), *Pustimarga and Sri Vallabhacarya,* Butala and Co., Delhi.

Van Buitenen, J.A.B. (1968), *Ramanuja on the Bhagavad-Gita*, Motilal Banarsidass, Delhi.

Van Buitenen, J.A.B. (1968), *Ramanuja Vedanta Sangraha,* Deccan College, Yervada, Poona.

Varadachari, K.C. (1969), *Ramanuja's Theory of Knowledge*, Chakravarthy Publication, Tirupati.

Varadachari, K.C. (1969), *Visistadvaita and its Development,* Chakravarthy Publication, Tirupati.

Varadachari, K.C. (1977), *Sri Ramanuja's Philosophy and Religion*, Rangacharya Memorial Trust, Madras.

Veliath, S.J. Cyril (1993), *The Mysticism of Ramanuja*, Munshiram Manoharlal Publishers Pvt. Ltd., Delhi.

Verma, H.N. & Verma, Amit (1975), *100 Great Indians Through the Ages*, GIP Books, Campbell, California, USA.

Vidyarthi, P.B. (1978), *Knowledge, Self and God in Ramanuja*, Orient Longman, New Delhi.

Vidyarthi, P.B. (1977), *Sri Ramanuja's Philosophy and Religion: A Critical Exposition of Visistadvaita*, Prof. M. Rangacharya Memorial Trust Triplicane, Madras.

Vivekananda, Swami (2001), *Bhakti Yoga: The Yoga of Love and Devotion,* Advaita Ashrama, Calcutta.

Vivekananda, Swami (2002), *Practical Vedanta,* Advaita Ashrama, Kolkata.

Vivekananda, Swami (2002), *Jnana Yoga: The Yoga of Knowledge,* Advaita Ashrama, Kolkata.

Vivekananda, Swami (2002), *Karma Yoga: The Yoga of Action*, Advaita Ashrama, Kolkata.

Vyas, R.N. (1990), Religion, Devotion and the Acharyas, Amar Prakashan, New Delhi.

Vyas, R.N. (1977), *The Bhagavata Bhakti Cult and Three Acharyas: Sankara, Ramanuja, and Vallabha,* Nag Publishers, Delhi.

Wilkins, William J. (1901), *Modern Hinduism,* Thacker, Spink and Company, London.

Williams, Monier (1891), *Brahmanism and Hinduism or Religious Thought and Life in India as Based on the Veda and Other Sacred Books of the Hindus,* John Murray, London.

Williams, Monier (1974), *Religious Thought and Life in India: Vedism, Brahmanism and Hinduism,* Munshiram Manoharlal Publishers Pvt. Ltd., New Delhi.

Williams, Sir Monier Monier (1971), *Hinduism*, Rare Books, Delhi.

Wilson, H.H. (1861), *A Sketch of the Religious Sects of the Hindus*, Cosmos Publications, New Delhi.

Wilson, H.H. (1972) (ed.) Ernst R. Rost (1972), *Religious Sects of the Hindus,* Indological Book, New Delhi.

Yati, Sri Bhakti Prajnana (1998), *Lord Sri Chaitanya and His Mission*, Sri Chaitanya Math, Nadia, W.B.

Zaehner, R.C. (1962), *Hinduism,* Oxford University Press, London.

Zimmer, Heinrich (1951), *Philosophers of India,* (eds. by Joseph Campbell), Routledge, Delhi.

Journal Articles

Williams, Monier (1881), *Indian Theistic Reformers*, (eds.), *Journal of the Asiatic Society*, London.

Sukhtankar, *Teachings of Vedanta According to Ramanuja,* Vienna Oriental Journal, Vol. XXII, pp. 128-29.

Newspapers Articles

Bhagavad Darshan (Ratha Yatra Aur Srichaitanya Mahaprabhu), *Hare Krishna Andolan Magazine*, June, 2003.